USING THINKING SKILLS IN THE PRIMARY CLASSROOM

USING THINKING SKILLS IN THE PRIMARY CLASSROOM

Peter Kelly

Paul Chapman Publishing

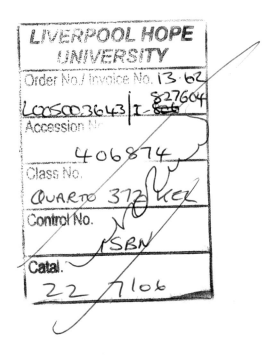
First published 2005

P·C·P

Paul Chapman Publishing
A SAGE Publications Company
1 Oliver's Yard
55 City Road
London EC1Y 1SP

SAGE Publications Inc.
2455 Teller Road
Thousand Oaks, California 91320

SAGE Publications India Pvt Ltd
B-42, Panchsheel Enclave
Post Box 4109
New Delhi 110 017

Library of Congress Control Number: 2004096202

A catalogue record for this book is available from the British Library

ISBN 1 4129 0015 8
ISBN 1 4129 0016 6 (pbk)

Typeset by Pantek Arts Ltd, Maidstone, Kent
Printed in Great Britain by The Cromwell Press, Melksham, Wilts

CONTENTS

ACKNOWLEDGEMENTS

I would like to thank the many colleagues and children with whom I have been fortunate to work and who have inspired me to write this book. Many of the case studies in the text stem from research which I have undertaken. As such specific participants cannot be named, but I thank them all for their contribution. Finally I thank my family for their patience.

Biographical Details

Peter Kelly is a Senior Lecturer on the Masters Degree programme at the Faculty of Education, University of Plymouth. Formerly he was head teacher of two schools in South West England – an inner city middle school and a village primary school. His teaching and research interests include learning through discourse, participatory assessment and democratic education. He is currently engaged in educational development activities in these areas as an educational consultant for UNICEF in Central Asia.

*F*IGURES

TASKS

Don't Think; Just Get on with Your Work!

The School Workplace

One of the joys of working with trainee teachers is the opportunity to visit them on placement in schools. On one such visit I had not left myself quite enough time to get to the school comfortably. I arrived with minutes to spare and was hurried to a classroom by the trainee's mentor. I was met by a confident and successful student teacher who was a model of efficiency and pace. She maintained a sense of purpose right from the start of the lesson, her instructions were clear and to the point, and whilst the children were involved in independent work she regularly monitored their progress and reminded the children several times of how long they had left to complete their task. Unlike me, she kept to her planned timings to the minute.

Later on that week I was visiting another student teacher in a class of 8 and 9-year-old children. He had set the children an individual writing task to complete, and was working with a small group of pupils when he looked across the classroom at a child who, despite having had five minutes to begin her work was not writing.

'Chloe, what are you doing?' he asked.

'Thinking, sir,' the girl replied.

'Well don't think,' he said, 'just get on with your work!'

These two events illustrate an underlying theme of this chapter: thinking time. We live in an impatient society dominated by notions of making good use of time. We dislike being kept waiting or spending too long on any one task, we are obsessed with doing things quickly and impatient for things to be done. It is no wonder that schools, mirroring society, are just the same.

Reflection Point

Thinking Time

Can you think of anything that is truly worthwhile which has been done quickly?

Although J.K. Rowling has been writing books about Harry Potter since 1994, the first was not published until 1997. In her fourth book she rewrote one particularly difficult chapter 13 times to get it right.

▶

Similarly, Vincent Van Gogh produced ten final paintings of sunflowers, and no doubt numerous other sketches and canvases on the way. But it is not just in the arts that things need time – the design and development of something new and innovative is often a long and protracted process.

James Dyson, the man who pioneered the 'bagless' vacuum cleaner, says he stumbled across the idea while renovating his country house in the Cotswolds. Noticing how vacuum cleaner bags clogged with dust, he set to work to try to resolve the problem. Five years and 5,127 prototypes later, he produced a model to revolutionize the vacuum cleaner market.

On a recent visit to a local glass factory I was impressed at the speed at which the glassblowers worked. However, although these craftspeople were able to make beautiful vases and bowls quickly, their craft had been developed over many years of apprenticeship and practice – we might consider the time committed during their apprenticeship as offsetting the time needed for their current craftwork. With finely tuned skills they can work efficiently and effectively, but I am sure that the designers of this glassware take considerably longer: despite their expertise, their creativity takes time here and now.

One of the most significant changes in industrial practices in the twentieth century came with the introduction of Henry Ford's production line. This arose from the need to meet the demand for motor cars in the USA, which was increasing at a phenomenal rate. In 1913 Ford introduced a continuous moving assembly line: workers remained in one place, adding one component to each car as it moved past them on the line. Work tasks were simple, requiring few skills and little knowledge. Parts were delivered to the workers by conveyor belt, carefully timed to keep the assembly line moving smoothly and efficiently. Ford controlled the production rate, and all workers had to work at the same speed. Ford calculated this speed through time and motion studies examining each individual task.

Ford's approach attempted to ensure maximum efficiency on the production line and to minimize waste, but his approach brought many problems. Workers were banned from talking and whispering, as Ford believed that this distracted them from the job and would reduce efficiency. This coupled with the unpleasant monotony of assembly-line work and Ford's repeated increases in the production targets assigned to workers, made illness and absenteeism commonplace. Further, he hired and fired as he pleased, creating an uneasy, untrusting and unmotivated workforce: by early 1914 the rate of employee turnover in his factory was between 40 and 60 per cent per month. Do you detect any parallels here with education?

Some industrialists realized that they were not making good use of their employees' talents. New approaches recognized, amongst other things, the need for employees to be treated like people and not machines. Indeed, tedious tasks were often carried out by machines and automated robots – designed, managed, built and looked after by an increasingly skilled workforce. Thus skills based training was considered essential. Further, employees were involved in decision-making, evaluating and planning for improvement, and were provided with opportunities to be innovative and creative. In short, they were trusted to do their work well and expected to be thoughtful and flexible. As a result they felt greater ownership of their work, were empowered to do their job well and showed increased job satisfaction and pride. So, in one European example of new industrial production methods, workers were organized in self-directing teams requiring very little management. They were asked to take on greater responsibility and given control of their own budgets. Once the slight workforce resistance and a lack of employee skills had been addressed, overall costs went down and productivity improved as people became more careful with expenditure, reduced wasteful practices, accepted more responsibility for their own practices and became more adaptive to changes.

Like Ford, schools have also faced the need to increase production (that is, raise standards) with an eye to effectiveness and efficiency, and to achieve this they have increasingly adopted production-line approaches to teaching and learning. The classroom has become a continuously moving production line: children have little freedom in directing their own learning; on the contrary, lessons structure learning. Learning objectives focus teaching on specific knowledge, taught in a specific order, addressing one component at a time, with mastery of previous learning a requirement for progress on to the next. Tasks are straightforward, clear and carefully timed to keep lessons moving smoothly and efficiently. On many occasions all children in a class are expected to work at the same speed – but this speed is constantly being increased by ever-moving targets for achievement in end of key stage tests. The result: for some the unpleasant monotony of assembly-line school work, an increase in illness (and, worryingly, mental illness) and absenteeism, and in some cases pupils who are uneasy, untrusting and unmotivated – having little understanding of the real purpose of their education.

As a prompt to help you reflect on your own practice and educational setting in relation to the industrial models described above, look at the statements in Task I.1. Whilst you are considering each pair of statements, reflect on where you feel your ideal practice lies, and whether external pressures cause you to adopt practices which you feel less happy with – how might you resist such pressures? You might also like to ask how useful it is to make a comparison with these industrial models: do they indeed provide useful metaphors for some aspects of school life? As with any such comparisons it is important to remember the limits to their usefulness: we can overgeneralize and read too much into them if we are not careful! However, they can allow us to see our practice and workplace from a new perspective, which is useful in helping identify areas for development.

Few would deny that teachers had a tough time during the reform-filled final decade of the twentieth century, and to some extent this continues, although the intensity of reform has perhaps reached a plateau. Little wonder, then, that teachers should strive to return to teaching that which they value. Concerns with the current situation are ever present in the educational media, and many headteachers are working to escape the clutches of the production-line curriculum. In this climate, a number of thoughtful approaches to curriculum design have proven extremely popular, and it is some of these, encompassed within the teaching thinking movement, to which I will now turn.

The Rise of the Teaching Thinking Movement

Teaching thinking is an umbrella term used to describe a range of approaches and programmes. Some, such as Reuven Feuerstein's 'Instrumental Enrichment' and its UK offshoot, the 'Somerset Thinking Skills Course', are context independent in that they aim to develop students' generic thinking skills though separate teaching programmes. Others, such as the cognitive acceleration family of programmes developed by Phil Adey and Michael Shayer at Kings College, London, are subject based in science, mathematics and, most recently, technology. In these, thinking skills are developed through subject teaching. Finally there are infusion programmes, where

Task 1.1 Your workplace metaphor

Look at these statements relating the industrial production line to the more recent 'self-directing teams' organizational structure. Such manufacturing models do not apply directly to schools, but can be considered as metaphors for schooling. Consider each pair of statements and reflect on your own professional circumstances and practice. Write any observations you have in the middle column. You might like to consider whether external pressures push you in particular directions and where you would like to be in an ideal world.

Industrial production line	Your professional circumstances	Self-directing teams
The focus is on attaining maximum efficiency and effectiveness in delivering an identical product		The focus is on increasing productivity without compromising the quality of the products
Production is carefully timed by managers to keep the assembly line moving smoothly and efficiently		The organization of production is flexible and under constant review by team members
Managers control the production rate, and all workers are expected to work at the same speed		Responsibility for the control and co-ordination of production is located with the teams of people who do the work
Production is planned in detail. Tasks exist in isolation and are not viewed as part of the whole manufacturing process		Production responds to customer need. Teams constantly seek to improve processes and products, in line with customer expectations Teams have a holistic view of production
Workers remain in one place, and work is carried out individually, with each worker accountable for the amount of work they do		Employees work in collaborative teams, rotating roles regularly. Teams accountable for the amount and quality of work
Workers cannot talk because this will distract them from the job and reduce efficiency		The social processes of groups are utilized to generate commitment to improvement and the creative involvement of all in the solution of problems
Tasks for workers required them to add one component to each car as it moved past them on the line at a time		Teams complete a whole section of the production process, and each team member becomes expert in all aspects so that they can support improvement
Work tasks are simple and repetitive. Everything required to do the work is provided by the manager on a conveyor belt		Work tasks are skilled and team members select appropriate raw materials and tools to improve productivity and quality
Workers have no say in improving the manufacturing process		Employees are partners in evaluating and improving the manufacturing process and working towards the organization's vision
Many workers find work monotonous, unfulfilling and therefore stressful		Many employees find the work challenging and fulfilling, and are committed to the organization's goals

Using Thinking Skills in the Primary Classroom © Kelly, 2005

both subject learning objectives and thinking skills learning objectives are addressed in the same lesson. One example is Steve Higgins's 'Thinking through Primary Teaching' programme.

In recent years such programmes have attracted considerable attention. Interest amongst headteachers and the educational media has been accompanied by increased government interest: reference to thinking skills in the 1997 white paper, 'Excellence in Schools' was followed in 1999 by a research report into approaches to teach thinking written by Carol McGuinness. This interest resulted in the inclusion of thinking skills in the revised National Curriculum for England in 1999.

There are many reviews of these programmes, and it is not my intention to consider them here, other than to make some points about their contribution to schools. I have little doubt that such programmes have been immensely worthwhile. Indeed, simply by encouraging teachers and children to focus on thinking they have repositioned the learner as central to the curriculum, following a long period where learning was marginalized and the management of teaching reigned supreme. In this their aims have resonated with practitioners concerned with the standards-driven reforms of the 1990s.

However there are assumptions made by many of those in the thinking skills movement with which I disagree. I will explore these differences and their significance for the approaches adopted in this book by considering two key questions: are there general thinking skills or only subject-specific ones; and can we teach thinking or is it more a matter of engaging students?

General or Subject-Specific Skills

Teaching thinking programmes aim to improve children's thinking. In this, some give the sense that they view thinking as physical exercise and the brain as a muscle: the more you exercise your brain by thinking, the fitter it will become to tackle harder thoughts. More sophisticated notions regard the performances of thinkers as those of sportspeople: learning particular rules, techniques and skills, practising them regularly and using them occasionally in authentic situations (that is, in competitions) will develop expert performance, and the features developed will, to some extent, transfer to other sports and to life beyond. In these views thinking people are like fit people: better able to tackle head-on what the world has to throw at them! I will show in the next chapter that this is also the view of some children.

Another common view sees thinking skills as collectable items which we can acquire at school, put in our 'learning bags' and take away with us. When we need these skills we simply go to our bags, take them out and use them. Of course, such a view belies the complexity of learning and thinking and their contextual nature. In this book I take the view that breaking thinking down into separate skills is not always helpful because – whether the metaphor is skill transfer or taking a tool out of a bag – this suggests that how we think has little relation to what we are thinking about: the way in which we use a tool depends as much (if not more) on the job we want to do and the circumstances in which we want to do it. More often it is better to view thinking as a whole, inseparable from the web of goals, ideas and social relations in which it happens. Thus I seldom refer to individual thinking skills out of context, and treat the terms 'using thinking skills' and 'engaged in deep thinking' synonymously.

It is useful to recognize that deep thinking is purposeful. Purposes can include searching for meaning, making critical judgements, being creative, problem-solving and decision-making.

Figure I.1 identifies some of the thinking activities involved in purposeful thinking. It is these thinking activities that some of the programmes mentioned above would describe as the general thinking skills we should help children to develop. I prefer to see them as prompts for teachers to use when planning activities to engage children's deep thinking in different areas of learning, and throughout this book I will identify opportunities to do this. I would argue that it is important to encourage children to, for example, solve problems in mathematics because this will help them learn and understand mathematics better and perhaps be more able to use their mathematics in new situations. However, and this is where the approach in this book differs from some in the teaching thinking movement, I would add that engaging in problem-solving in mathematics does not help children develop general problem-solving skills which would allow them to solve problems in other areas of learning such as science or technology. The skill of mathematical problem-solving is closely related to solving problems using mathematics.

Thinking purpose	Related thinking activities
Searching for meaning	Sequencing, ordering, ranking Sorting, classifying, grouping Analysing, parts-whole, compare-contrast, similarities and differences
Making critical judgements	Making predictions, hypothesizing Drawing conclusions, reasons for conclusions Distinguishing fact from opinion Determining bias, reliability of evidence Relating cause and effect, designing a fair test
Being creative	Generating ideas and possibilities Building and combining ideas Formulating own points of view Taking multiple perspectives and seeing others' points of view
Problem-solving	Identifying problems Thinking up different solutions Testing out solutions Planning
Decision-making	Making decisions Generating options Weighing up pros and cons Reviewing consequences

Figure I.1 Thinking purposes and activities

Teaching or Engaging Thinking

Do children need to learn to think or can they think already? Some thinking skills programmes are influenced by the views of Piaget, who asserted that children's thinking goes through a series of qualitative changes as they grow and develop. However, such ideas have been challenged by research which views the learner as an inseparable part of a social situation, and some now believe the thinking processes of children to be exactly the same as those of adults: what children lack is experience and knowledge.

My own view is that some have mistakenly identified children's 'lack of engagement' as an 'inability to think', and that approaches such as those adopted in many teaching thinking programmes have simply engaged children's existing thinking, rather than taught them to think. This book adopts a different metaphor: a visual one. We can all think. Like seeing, it is part of being human, and like seeing, unless we have a specific difficulty to overcome we do not need to learn to do it better. But thinking has to be thinking about something, and the more you know about something and the more experience you have of using those particular ideas and relating them to the world, then the better you will be able to make sense of the world with them. When we think in particular ways and use particular tools we come to see the world in different ways, and we notice and attend to different things. We might see the world as a poet, as a mathematician, as a scientist or as a painter. In seeing the world in these ways we become able to express our experiences as a poet or painter, and explore our understandings of the world as a mathematician or scientist. In this, seeing the world as a scientist and being a scientist are one of the same thing.

Many of the common characteristics of thinking skills programmes also feature prominently in this book: using co-operative learning; encouraging talk; promoting challenge; working in subject domains; encouraging transfer; and stimulating pupils to think about their learning. But they are adopted here to enable children to use their thinking to come to see and make sense of the world in different ways. Seeing the world through different eyes, such as those of the academic disciplines, provides the 'ends' of education: thinking is the 'means' to those ends. This book is about using children's thinking skills in the primary classroom.

Children Are Thinkers

As a teacher I was confronted daily with children engaged in amazingly sophisticated thinking. Unfortunately this thinking seldom related directly to the school curriculum. Take this example of a conversation between two 11-year-old girls about their previous night's viewing of a popular soap opera on television:

Jasmine: Do you think Scott should leave Claire?

Tania: Well, no, it's his fault really. He should have spent more time with her and taken her out more. She was lonely, because he was working so much. She just wanted company. He's got his job, but she hasn't got anything else.

Jasmine: So why didn't she tell him she was lonely?

Tania: I guess she was cross with him and wanted to get back at him.

Jasmine: But he had to work hard so they could buy a house. It wasn't just his fault. I think Claire felt guilty about being upset because he worked so much, and now things are even worse because he's upset with her as well.

These children consider a complex moral question from the two perspectives of Scott and Claire. They show considerable sensitivity to the characters' relationship difficulties, and negotiate an answer to a question by considering both points of view and coming to a conclusion.

Reflection Point

The Expert Mechanic

Many years ago I taught at a school situated in an area of considerable social disadvantage. I had had to nip out of school one lunchtime to visit the bank, and as I drove back onto the school site I could see a 9-year-old boy who was in my class watching me from the corner of the school field nearest to the car park.

After lunch he came into class and told me that he had heard my car engine misfire as I accelerated away from school at the start of lunch, but that it seemed okay when I drove slowly into the car park on my return. He went on to tell me that there were a number of things which could be wrong with my car. As the car was misfiring when cold it could be that my spark plugs might need replacing. However, the engine started easily, which he would not expect if the plugs were at fault. He then said that it could be a fuel problem, but most misfiring problems were in fact electrical. Finally, he concluded that it was most likely that the fault lay with the ignition wires or distributor, and that I should get these checked. Sure enough, when I visited a garage later that day I was told that the ignition wires did indeed need replacing, as there was a short circuit from one of them.

What made my earlier conversation all the more interesting was that this boy could read at the level of a 6-year-old and write very little indeed, apart from his name. He had significant learning difficulties when it came to these, yet he could express himself so clearly in the area of 'engine troubleshooting'. Further, like the girls in the previous example, he could consider the solution to a problem from a number of perspectives, using evidence to make inferences based on his knowledge of how an engine works. This had been learned whilst helping his father who owned a local garage but who spent a good deal of his spare time working on cars at his home. The knowledge he had gained from this apprenticeship with his father had taken him towards becoming an expert problem-solver in car mechanics – at 9 years of age!

Research has supported the conclusion that children can and often do engage in extremely sophisticated thinking. For example, in one well-known study by Terezinha Nunes and her colleagues in the 1980s, the mathematical competences of Brazilian street children were examined. These children were street traders who had to purchase goods from various wholesalers, price the goods and then sell them. The mathematics involved was complex, especially as Brazil's rate of inflation at the time was 250 per cent per annum – and had to be accounted for by the children. The children, only one of whom had been at formal school for more than four years, were observed to achieve a 98 per cent overall success rate in making these extremely complex calculations in their day-to-day trading activities. Interestingly, the study also found that the children were unable to use these mathematical competences when taken into an academic environment: their ability to do these calculations depended as much on the context in which they were needed and which gave them meaning. As in the previous examples, meaningful real problems are understandable to children in ways in which the artificial problems of schooling sometimes are not.

The examples above suggest that many children already have a considerable range of thinking skills and are able to think in sophisticated ways. But how can we know what our children are thinking? Try Task I.2 in your classroom.

Task I.2 How do we know what children are thinking?

Observe an individual child working with a group of other children on a task. Note any actions or talk which you feel might give a clue to what the child is thinking. How can you be sure that this is the case, that you are actually getting at the child's thinking? How might you verify your presumptions?

I'm sure that you will agree that it is very difficult to deduce what is going on inside someone's head from what they say and do. Sometimes a child who appears to be working by trial and error is actually following a strategy which the observer has failed to recognize. Children's comments can be misinterpreted and misunderstood because they lack the clarity and detail which would allow their significance to be recognized by the observer. Often when looking at children working in groups it is hard to separate one person's contribution from another. Look again at the conversation at the start of this section: who contributed more; which child was most thoughtful; could either child have made such thoughtful contributions without the other; did they, in fact, support each other to think at a level which they would have found difficult to do alone? If you can arrange joint observations it is useful to compare your observations with those of a colleague, an exercise which often reveals significant differences of interpretation.

Individual or group interviews can be helpful in revealing children's thinking. Try Task I.3 on the next page.

Now choose one or two of the more skilful hobbies for each child and ask them to tell you:

- What things have you done recently in relation to that hobby?

- What do you find most interesting about that hobby?

- What is it about that hobby that you like? What do you find difficult?

- If I wanted to start that hobby what would I need to do, know and understand?

- In what ways are you better at that hobby now than you were a few months ago? What has changed? What helped you get better?

Look through their answers for thoughtful examples, and any unexpected responses. How does this perspective on the child compare to that which you have gained in school?

However, again we must be cautious: children often say what they think their teacher would like them to say. They try to guess the 'right answer'. Thus children's comments in this task might not reflect their thinking about their hobbies; rather they might be an indication of what they think makes you (their teacher) happy. Of course, this is the case in all teacher-initiated discussions.

Bearing such limitations in mind, I hope you will still find enough evidence to be convinced that many children already have a considerable range of thinking skills and are able to think in sophisticated ways. If this is the case, then our challenge as educators lies in engaging that thinking and using it to support their learning. This is the theme of the rest of this book.

Task I.3 Children are thinkers

Ask a small number of children whether they have any hobbies, interests or belong to any groups, and complete the table below for each child.

	Examples
Art or craft based	
Sporting (personal involvement, not just spectating)	
Naturalist, animals, collection based	
Musical	
Pen friends, letter-writing, cubs or brownies	
Keeping a diary, photograph album	
Sunday School, church, and so on	
Writing, for example poetry, fiction	
Puzzles, quizzes, competitions	
Reading, cinema, watching television, theatre	
Other clubs and interests	

Using Thinking Skills in the Primary Classroom © Kelly, 2005

Using Thinking Skills in the Primary Classroom

In this introductory chapter I have argued that children are thinkers, but that there are schooling barriers to engaging this thinking. Chapter 1 considers these barriers in more detail and provides some ideas about how children learn in schools and what factors we must consider if we are to improve their engagement and promote greater use of these thinking skills.

In the remainder of the book we consider opportunities to move towards greater pupil engagement in primary schools. Chapter 2 considers the use of discourse and group work to remove the barriers to engagement, and Chapter 3 looks at how assessment, which has a huge influence over all aspects of classroom life including, unsurprisingly, the approaches pupils adopt to their learning, can be used to promote the use of thinking skills.

Chapter 4 describes how schooling structures children's thinking, and how this can be used in positive ways by, for example, helping children to see the world as a mathematician, a poet and so on. It also considers the value of considering the same themes from several different perspectives to enrich learning, including 'real-life' contexts of use. Complementing this, Chapter 5 considers how we can encourage children to step outside the boxes which structure their thinking, and to think creatively.

Finally, Chapter 6 addresses the issues surrounding the development of a whole-school approach to issues of engagement and thinking, that is, to those of developing a thinking school.

A Note about the Format and Content of This Book

Chapter 6 argues that thinking schools need thinking teachers – and children need models of deep thinking if they too are to engage in deep thinking. Such teachers, who adopt what I will call in Chapter 6 a deep professionalism, focus on understanding and improving student learning.

This book aims to encourage deep professionalism, whether it is used for personal reflection or as a basis for whole-school in-service training (INSET). Thus it adopts a style which attempts to be challenging and illustratory. It does not provide simply tips, pro formas and lesson plans, all of which can easily be purchased elsewhere and are instantly available on the Internet. However, as well as 'Tasks' and 'Reflection Points' such as those which you have met already in this introduction, I include practical examples and boxes of 'Lesson Ideas' and 'Good Practice Points' throughout the text. Where appropriate, the thinking skills emphasis of activities is also included.

Key Points

1. Schools have increasingly lost the human touch and become 'knowledge factories'. Unfortunately this has led to a focus on teaching and management at the expense of learning.

2. By focusing on certain measurable learning outcomes, the quality of children's deep learning and understanding has been largely ignored. An unplanned outcome to this has been a lack of engagement by children in their learning at schools. However, there are many out of school contexts in which children engage, develop and use their thinking.

3. The thinking skills movement has been immensely worthwhile by encouraging teachers to reposition learners and learning at the centre of the curriculum. Proponents claim that the approach has taught children to think. It is my view in this book that in many such cases children have simply begun to use their existing thinking capabilities.

4. Schools are often structured in ways which stop children from thinking, and children often comply by choosing not to think in school. These barriers are discussed in Chapter 1. Useful approaches to engaging children's exsiting thinking relating to dialogue and assessment are considered in Chapters 2 and 3.

5. Chapter 4 considers how we can best support the development of children's structured thinking, whilst creativity is considered in Chapter 5.

6. This book provides a whole-school resource which could be used as a basis for staff development. The final chapter draws ideas together for whole-school approaches to engaging, using and developing thinking in the primary school.

CHAPTER 1

A Place to Think

Schools as 'Thinking-free Zones'

Children are thinkers, as I have illustrated in the introduction to this book. Like adults, they are able to think in quite sophisticated ways. Indeed, some would suggest that there is little qualitative difference between the thinking of children and that of adults, although there are significant differences between the thinking of novices and experts, whether they are children or adults. But despite their abilities to think, children choose not to think in schools, and in this chapter I suggest why this might be and what we can do about it.

Reflection Point

Children's Views About School Work

Why is it that many children do not, as a matter of course, think about their school work? What is it about schools that stop children thinking? A few years ago I carried out a study exploring primary children's experiences of learning mathematics at school. The findings were revealing. I deliberately chose to interview only high-attaining 11-year-old pupils whom their teacher had identified as being articulate and confident. Again and again children's responses to my questions about the mathematics they were doing in school focused on their role in doing work, without considering the actual tasks they were involved in or their thinking about these. Anna's comment, when asked about what she was thinking when doing some mathematics, was typical: 'I wasn't thinking anything, I was just doing it.'

For many of the children involved, doing mathematics is doing mental work. Thus they suggested that to make mathematics harder you use bigger numbers. After a rest (when you play and have fun) you feel refreshed, but need to get used to doing mental work again. Sometimes after a long rest you need to warm your brain up, doing easier work first. Adam expressed this view most clearly:

> We did that work to get your numbers working because you might have lost your numbers in your head over the holiday because you need to refresh your memory. I had to refresh my memory because over the holiday I wasn't doing much number work, I was just doing like fun things because it was quite sunny. It got harder as you got further on, the bigger the number the harder it gets. You make it harder by putting higher numbers. On the division it was harder because there was more to do.

Similarly, in relation to learning, some children expressed the view that the harder your brain works, the more good it does you. This is because you will become more able to do work easily and thus become quicker at working. This mirrors directly physical exercise, and includes a belief that success is down to getting right answers as quickly as possible: As Daniel puts it:

> You could have made it a lot harder and then that would have been more mind-bending and it would make your brain work a lot harder. If you always do easy work then it isn't really going to get you anywhere, and if you make it harder it helps you learn and do things more quickly.

Many of these children were working without a personal purpose: they simply focused on following the instructions provided by their teacher. So, when asked about a lesson which I had observed, Anna commented, 'we had to do the five times table down there, I don't know why, it's just maths – it was just some maths we had to do'.

Comments such as these suggest that the production line is more than an interesting metaphor for describing busy and industrious classrooms: it literally reflects many children's lived experiences of classrooms.

Approaches to Learning

Before considering children's approaches to learning it might be helpful to think about our own. As a starting point, look at Task 1.1 (next page) and try to identify what you do in each of the three learning situations.

The children in the previous section all described their learning in a particular way – as work. We might say that they all adopted a similar approach to learning. Some researchers have studied the approaches to learning which people adopt in different learning situations. Focusing on students in higher education, Noel Entwistle[1] described three levels at which students engage with their learning: deep, surface and strategic. The characteristics of each approach are summarized in Figure 1.1.

Deep	Surface	Strategic
Learner's intention: To understand ideas for yourself	*Learner's intention:* To cope with the course requirements	*Learner's intention:* To achieve the highest possible grades
Features of the learner's approach: Relates ideas to previous knowledge and experience	*Features of the learner's approach:* Studies without reflecting on either purpose or strategy	*Features of the learner's approach:* Puts consistent effort into studying
Looks for patterns and underlying principles	Treats the course as unrelated bits of knowledge	Finds the right conditions and materials for studying
Checks evidence and relates it to conclusions	Memorizes facts and procedures routinely	Is alert to assessment requirements and criteria
Examines logic and argument cautiously and critically	Finds difficulty in making sense of new ideas presented	Gears work to the perceived preferences of lecturers
Becomes actively interested in the course content	Feels undue pressure and worry about work	Manages time and effort effectively

Figure 1.1 Defining features of approaches to learning

Task 1.1 How do we approach learning?

In each of the following learning situations, which of the statement pairs is your preferred approach closer to?

In lectures do you focus on:

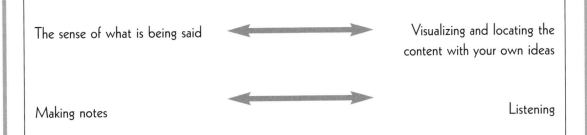

The sense of what is being said	Visualizing and locating the content with your own ideas
Making notes	Listening

When revising do you prefer to:

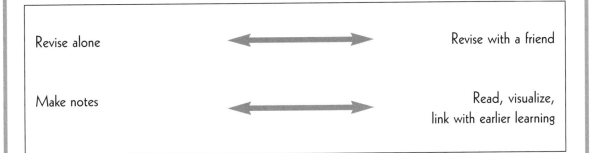

Revise alone	Revise with a friend
Make notes	Read, visualize, link with earlier learning

When reading a difficult research article would you:

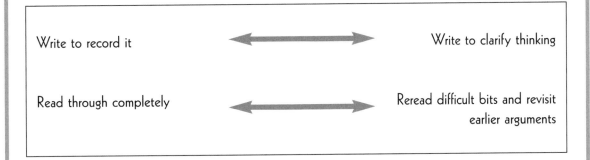

Write to record it	Write to clarify thinking
Read through completely	Reread difficult bits and revisit earlier arguments

Using Thinking Skills in the Primary Classroom © Kelly, 2005

If you return to the statements in Task 1.1 you will see that those on the right characterize a deep approach to learning, whilst those on the left characterize a surface one. Did you find that your responses fell predominantly on one side or the other? It may be that your approach depends on the type of situation – not everyone likes attending lectures and some prefer to study alone. Further, if we feel under pressure or that outcomes are more significant than understanding, we might be more inclined to adopt surface approaches: as a teacher on an assessment training course once said, 'I don't want a lot of theory, I don't want to work things out for myself – just tell me how to do it!'

Although Entwistle's work was carried out with adult learners, similar views have been expressed by researchers working with younger learners.[2] In one, Carl Bereiter identified two ways in which children relate to school work. The first marginalizes learning, making it no more than coincidental to school work, with children focusing on work, activities, completion and production rate. However, in the second, learning is central and understanding is pursued.

These approaches are, of course, closely aligned to the level of student thinking and engagement. Those adopting deep and strategic approaches to learning are engaging with their learning in a thoughtful way, and if we are to promote these then we must explore the factors which influence learners to adopt these approaches. In the following sections I will consider why children acquire particular approaches to learning, first by looking at the factors which influence them and, secondly, by asking if particular learners have a tendency to adopt particular approaches.

What We Learn Is Linked to How We Learn

An often overlooked, but nevertheless crucially important perspective on learning is that of the learner. So often we make assumptions about what learners need, what their difficulties are, and how these can be overcome without asking the learners themselves. Try Task 1.2 with a small group of children – and be prepared for some surprises!

Task 1.2 Purposeful learning?

Talk to a small group of children about their learning at school. Ask the following questions:

> Why do you think you come to school?
> Why do we have to work at school?
> What are the things we do at school for?
> Tell me about some of the things you did yesterday?
> Why do you think you did each of those things?
> How might the things you did yesterday help you today in school? How might they help you next term? How about next year?
> How will the things you do at school help you when you are an adult?

Consider the children's answers. Were you surprised by any of them? What were the similarities and differences between what individual children said? How aware were the children of the intended purposes of their school work?

Ask children in any English primary school why they think they learn a subject like mathematics at school and I would put money on the following being the most common responses: to get better at maths; to help me when I am doing maths later on; to help me pass tests; and to help me when I get to secondary school. Occasionally children link their learning of mathematics to use in out of school situations, but when they do the mathematics is very simple: counting, shopping and measurement! Rarely do children see mathematics as being a 'uniquely powerful set of tools to understand and change the world'.[3] To what extent does this mirror your findings in Task 1.2?

Let us stay with mathematics for a short while to illustrate the effect assessment can have on children's learning. Of course, the testing stakes are high for children. Pressure is put on them by schools through the use of extra classes to 'boost' their performance, revision materials and homework, teaching that continually asserts the importance of tests and so on. Indeed, in England the national testing experience at the end of year 6 has become a ritual rite of passage for many 11-year-olds at the culmination of their primary schooling. It is inevitable that children will notice the importance placed upon tests, and that this will influence their views of learning.

It is therefore not surprising when, no matter how well we teach mathematics, children see most of their mathematics as being of little value to them beyond school success or testing, and thus remain unable to use their learning outside school. Being tied so closely to 'performance' in school, their mathematical knowledge becomes largely inert away from school. Indeed, performance reflects well another barrier to deep learning in schools: approaches such as the National Numeracy Strategy focus so much on performance, with teachers relishing their pupils' demonstrations of how quickly and how efficiently they can do complex but routine problems (such as mental calculations), that they ignore deeper learning.

Reflection Point

Testing Troubles

The effects of test-led curricula on learning are well documented in the findings of educational researchers: many studies have shown that people can be (and often are) very successful at passing examinations without developing a deep (or transferable) understanding of an area of knowledge. Ference Marton, the Swedish educationalist, provides an extreme example of this, where physics graduates with first class honours degrees were shown to be unable to apply their expertise to everyday physics situations (such as the behaviour of the level of liquid in a glass of wine on a table in an accelerating train). Indeed, it is worth asking how many of us can recall much of the learning acquired for examinations that we have taken in the past?

The National Numeracy Strategy describes numeracy (in its Foreword) as 'a key life skill', and adds 'without basic numeracy skills, our children will be disadvantaged throughout life'. The word 'skill' is important because it implies that such an ability is unproblematically transferable from one context, the context of learning, to another, the context of application. This agrees closely with the Cockroft Report's view, over 15 years previously, describing numeracy as the ability to use mathematical skill to enable individuals to cope with the practical mathematics of everyday life. But much mathematics teaching in English primary schools attempts simply to develop children's ability to carry out calculations involving number (a lesser aim than Cockroft's 'use mathematical skill') in a variety of almost entirely schooling contexts as measured almost entirely through national tests. Rarely are contexts from everyday life or methods of appraising children's performance other than testing included. It is really little wonder that our children find the use and application of mathematics so difficult.

Many factors influence the learner's experience of and engagement with their learning, and although little research has focused on primary aged children, the findings of studies of older learners illuminate some of the influences younger learners face. Not only overbearing assessment systems which emphasize testing, but also highly intensive and fast-moving courses, content-filled curricula and an overuse of 'knowledge transmission' teaching methods have all been linked strongly with the adoption by learners of surface approaches to learning.[4] This is unsurprising, and at best in such conditions we might encourage learners to become strategic rather than superficial in their learning. As this list encompasses the kind of regimes which decades of initiatives have encouraged in our primary schools, it is little wonder that so many children in them do not think about or engage with their learning. It seems obvious, therefore, to suggest that if we want to improve children's thinking in primary schools we should:

- move away from assessment regimes which are overdependent on testing (the focus of Chapter 3);

- focus on addressing key areas of learning in depth rather than providing pacey but superficial 'blanket' coverage of much larger areas (considered in Chapter 4);

- use a variety of teaching methods, emphasizing those which encourage student decision-making and active approaches to learning (as identified in Chapters 2 and 5).

I have much to say about these in the coming chapters.

The Role of Working Practices

Reflection Point

Children's Responses to Different Lessons

A few years ago I conducted a study into how the tasks in which children engage influence the approach which they adopt to learning in those tasks. Specifically I asked whether a primary pupil's learning about a particular theme or concept in history differs substantively if it occurs within the context of, say, a drama lesson than if it occurs within a literacy hour.

This has particular significance for primary teachers in England. Using highly detailed lesson planning, schools have attempted to develop schemes of work which not only present learning to children in an order and form which make sense to them, but which also allows all children access to all areas of learning in the National Curriculum whilst avoiding repetition. However, with the increasing focus on literacy and numeracy following the introduction of the National Literacy and Numeracy Strategies in 1998 and 1999 respectively, other subjects have had to compete for space within a content-packed curriculum. A key strategy for curriculum design, aiming to reduce content overload whilst providing access for every child to the full curriculum, has been the teaching of aspects of some subjects within others. For example, writing up science investigations might be taught within the National Literacy Strategy's 'literacy hour', history through sharing historical texts and collecting and analysing scientific data within a numeracy lesson focusing on data handling. Indeed, Her Majesty's Chief Inspector, David Bell, has suggested such an approach to tackle the poor state of teaching in the foundation subjects.

My study was conducted on the premise that, if the historical learning resulting from such experiences were qualitatively different from that resulting from other forms of curriculum presentation, then this would have serious implications for practitioners.

During a half-term period, year 6 children from four primary schools followed the same scheme of work for history, looking at the Saxons as an example of invaders and settlers. In this scheme, four lessons were identified for child post-task interviews:

- a literacy lesson based on a text on social and domestic arrangements in Saxon settlements, which also described the use of archaeological evidence;

- a history lesson in which the children used a selection of texts, provided by their teacher, to gather information about particular aspects of social life in Saxon times and the evidence for this, and used this information to create their own account;

- a drama lesson in which children developed ideas with their teacher whilst enacting roles set in a Saxon village;

- a historical enquiry in which the children handled genuine Saxon artefacts, and worked with an archaeologist to identify their function and properties.

Mostly the children adopted either or both of two approaches: at times they focused on trying to understand historical and other ideas in their lessons, and at other times they focused on the organizational aspects of their work and on meeting its requirements. All children adopted both deep and surface approaches, but the approach adopted together with the focus of their activity depended to some extent on the nature of the lesson they were involved in.

In a literacy lesson based on a historical text, the majority of children focused on a deep approach to the literacy aspects of learning, describing concerns with areas such as the authors' intentions and the layout and style of the text. They also readily identified new words, considering both their meaning and spelling. When describing the purpose of the work they suggested it was to develop their reading and listening skills. However, a quarter of the children focused only on meeting the assessment requirements of lessons and coping with the organizational aspects of the work – remembering what to do next and trying to finish in time for the end of the lesson. And only one child in ten focused on understanding the historical ideas presented in lessons. Thus we might suggest that presenting history as literacy encourages children to focus on their learning of literacy and not on historical skills and ideas. This has implications for the quality of history learning in primary schools if practitioners accept the proposal that, in order to rationalize the curriculum, history can, to some extent, be taught through literacy.

The complexity of the text-based research task seems to have had a dramatic effect on children's adopted approaches to learning in that lesson. Almost all of children's comments in relation to this lesson were surface, focusing on how they did the task, with little understanding of the reasons for their activity. The drama lesson was far more successful in enabling children to focus on their learning and understanding of history. Children described how this experience helped them to make links in their learning, both between areas of study within the unit on Saxons, across different units of history and with their present-day experiences. However, the task type most successful at promoting deep approaches to historical ideas was historical enquiry using original artefacts, with three-quarters of children focusing on understanding ideas relating to the lives of Saxons and the nature and use of historical evidence.

Certainly this study supports a balanced approach to teaching humanities subjects rather than the narrow one advocated by government advisers in England, and now adopted in many English primary schools. Although children should have opportunities to be taught one subject through another, this should not be their only experience. Indeed, whilst subjects benefit from being addressed as disciplines in their own right, much can also be gained by looking at conceptual areas through, for example, drama and literature: a combination of separate and combined approaches would seem to be most effective in encouraging deep learning.

This Reflection Point highlights the importance of the way in which learning is presented in encouraging deep learning. It seems that it is the way people work and the things they do which are crucial. Working practices are the 'taken for granted' ways of working which are implicit in our daily activities. For example, being a pupil in a school involves learning to perform (that is, work) well on school tasks within the context of schooling. In this context, the strategies or working practices which pupils often adopt include:

- using language which conforms to the required classroom conventions;

- producing work which is neat;

- reading the classroom and/or interpersonal cues available from teachers and other adults to predict a correct response when questioned;

- teaching the teacher what to expect from you – 'I only write half a page, and if you let me get away with this then I will co-operate with you';

- knowing and using the different 'pecking orders' within a class – 'I am no good at maths so I can be a "passenger" in whole-class mathematical discussions, but I am top of the class when it comes to being a clown – people expect me to be so';

- understanding the assessment systems within the classroom and putting one's energies into meeting these rather than spending too much time on things which are not assessed and therefore not rewarded;

- further to this, knowing what is important for success and learning it.

In short, being a pupil involves learning the working practices of schooling.

Sometimes children are even coached specifically in the working practices of testing, by being taught how to do better at tests. This might include understanding how tests are constructed (for example, 'if a question has three marks, then you need to make three points') or even learning pre-prepared phrases (such as 'the sun was shimmering like a piece of amber surrounded by blue topaz') which they could use in their narrative writing to impress the examiner!

Different approaches bring with them different working practices which have different effects on children. Thus the example in the preceding section of a text-based research task required overly complex working practices on the part of the children, and this detracted from their deep engagement with historical ideas. The working practices bulleted above would appear to pertain more to 'traditional' classrooms, whereas a different set of practices might be evident in a classroom organized for problem-based learning. As I described in the last section, 'traditional' working practices tend to focus children on the usefulness of their learning in testing contexts alone and this can result in knowledge which is inert in other application contexts. However, collaborative and problem-based learning working practices (which require flexibility and creativity, and are the subject of Chapter 2) result in learning which is seen by learners as useful in many contexts including both problem-solving and testing.

Clearly this last set of working practices is likely to encourage children's deep engagement with their learning: problem-oriented, collaborative classrooms which encourage flexible and creative approaches are likely to engage children's thinking skills.

Identity and Beliefs

We all have many identities which relate to the roles we adopt and the stances we take in different areas of our lives. These influence the way we go about things in those areas and beyond: my identity as a parent influences the way in which I respond not only to my own children, but to other peoples' children as well. Children have many identities as well, and some of these have already been explored in Task I.3 in the last chapter. At school we only see one (or at most a few) of the many ways children engage with the world – we see children somewhat one dimensionally rather than as multidimensional and complex individuals.

In an earlier section I suggested particular learners might have a tendency to adopt particular approaches to learning. This tendency can result from a learner's identity as a learner: how they see themselves and how they think others see them as a learner. Look at how children have described their involvement in different out-of-school activities in Task I.3. Do they represent themselves as learners in different activities in the same way?

Both in school and out, children have learning identities which can influence their approaches to learning. In school some learners see themselves as simply being receivers of knowledge: they like authoritative sources, whether these are teachers or textbooks, and they prefer right and wrong answers to shades of opinion. Such students like clear demonstrations of knowledge, skills or procedures which they can copy in order to learn. Other learners prefer to offer more of themselves to their learning – enjoying debate and discussion, with many perspectives and answers, and sometimes little or no consensus.

These identities have other facets. Whereas both received and discursive knowers can have a strong knowledge of the discipline they have learnt, discursive learners tend to be more flexible in their approach, and are more likely to reinterpret and be creative in their use of disciplinary ideas and procedures, which is helpful in problem-solving situations. Further, received knowers tend to resort to trial and error approaches to non-routine problems, whereas discursive knowers show greater resilience and resourcefulness: they have a degree of self-belief, a knowledge that most problems are solvable if looked at in the right way and a determination to get there in the end.

Such identities are not entirely fixed; they can be influenced by the practices which learners are exposed to in schools: the working practices of traditional classrooms encourage 'received knowers', whereas problem-based, collaborative and discursive classrooms encourage 'discursive knowers'. No doubt issues of motivation and peer interest play their part as well, which collaborative, discursive and problem-oriented classrooms can harness in order to develop positive learning identities. Think back to your own schooldays and complete Task 1.3 to provide an insight into how identity and learning related to each other for you.

Thus schools can have an enormous influence on children's identities as learners. But the identities which learners adopt are also influenced to a large extent by their beliefs about learning, and it is to these which I now turn.

Conceptions of Learning

Learning itself can be conceived of in a variety of ways. Some researchers have suggested a hierarchy of conceptions which learners can have of learning:[5]

Task 1.3 Exploring identity through reflections on schooldays

Think back to your own schooldays, the subjects (or aspects of subjects) you enjoyed and the choices you made. Reflect on the extent to which you liked the people who taught or took those subjects with you, the subjects themselves and the ways in which they were taught.

What was it that drew you towards making those choices?

Area of learning	Influence on choice		
	People	Subject	Teaching

Now consider the extent to which your choices reflected your identity (how you saw yourself and how you perceived others to see you), or was your identity to some extent changed by those choices?

Using Thinking Skills in the Primary Classroom © Kelly, 2005

- at the simplest level learning means increasing one's knowledge;

- slightly more complex is the notion of learning as memorizing and reproducing;

- at a slightly higher level is the view of learning as the ability to use and apply knowledge or procedures;

- at the next level, learning is understanding, which involves coming to see something in a particular way;

- in order to appreciate the world in new ways we have to adopt a view of learning as changing understanding.

The most sophisticated view, according to this perspective, sees learning as changing as a person: as learning involves changing the way we understand and see the world, in consequence it involves changing us as people, that is, changing our identities. So, for example, learning history involves becoming a historian. Being a historian involves seeing the world through a historian's eyes, and describing it thus: in challenging existing ways of doing this and providing new ways; in providing a greater understanding of humanity and fresh insights into what it is to be human. Being a historian involves seeing ourselves as historians and wanting others to see us as historians as well.

In considering Germany during the Second World War a historian might ask, 'What does the Holocaust tell us about the human experience or condition?' and, 'How can the Holocaust help us to understand the human experience or condition better?' This could be addressed by considering the role, knowledge and acquiescence of individual German citizens in the Holocaust and comparing it to that of the Nazi authorities. Fresh insights could therefore be gained by looking at these dreadful but familiar events in a new way – from the perspective of ordinary German citizens (as a result of asking a question about something that had not been explored before). Of course, such an academic study has been carried out, being the subject of the book *Hitler's Willing Executioners*.[6]

Further, the historian might consider the implications that the acquiescence of ordinary Germans in such a dreadful act have for our understanding of communities who, facing an influx of refugees, respond with violent rioting, and of governments who respond to such situations with 'assessment' or 'assimilation' centres and the like. Thus the historian uses the working practices of history to reach out and explore the world. Chapter 4 addresses this further, considering how we can develop a curriculum which encourages our children to become mathematicians, poets, geographers, historians and the like, and in doing so to also reach out and explore their worlds.

A Better Metaphor

So we return to the ways in which children perceive their classrooms. At the start of this chapter it was suggested that the production line is more than a metaphor for classroom life; it literally reflects many children's lived experiences of classrooms. In order to engage children's thinking skills in classrooms we need better metaphors: the poet's study, the artist's studio, the scientist's laboratory are possibilities, and there are many more.

Adopting such metaphors means redefining the purpose of our activities in schools. The current focus on teaching as the effective communication of particular knowledge as measured by standardized tests needs to be replaced by a focus on learning: learning which involves us reaching out to explore, describe and explain the world, and in doing so define our place in it. In such classrooms learners will draw on the ideas and practices of others who have sought to do the same, but will also make their own contribution. Such practices will help form their identities as people who see their place in the world in many ways, but who also have their own perspective bringing fresh thoughts and insights.

Key Points

1. The school production line is not just a metaphor for busy classrooms, for many children it is their lived experience of classrooms.

2. Production-line approaches encourage surface approaches to learning, but if we want learners to engage with their learning in a thoughtful way we need to:

    (a) move away from assessment regimes which are overdependent on testing;

    (b) focus on addressing key areas of learning in depth rather than providing pacey but superficial 'blanket' coverage of much larger areas;

    (c) use a variety of teaching methods, emphasizing those which encourage student decision-making and active approaches to learning;

3. A combination of separate and combined approaches would seem to be most effective in encouraging deep learning.

4. Problem-oriented, collaborative and discursive classrooms which encourage flexible and creative approaches are helpful in engaging children's thinking skills, including both problem-solving and testing.

5. Children have learning identities which can influence their approaches to learning:

    (a) 'received knowers' see themselves as simply being receivers of knowledge, and show little flexibility in using their knowledge, for example, tending to resort to trial and error approaches when tackling non-routine problems;

    (b) 'discursive knowers' prefer discursive, collaborative approaches, and show greater resilience and resourcefulness than 'received knowers'. they have a degree of self belief, a knowledge that most problems are solvable if looked at in the right way and show considerable determination

6. Learning identities are not entirely fixed, and schools can have an enormous influence on the identities children adopt as learners:

    (a) the practices of traditional classrooms encourage 'received knowers';

    (b) problem-oriented, collaborative and discursive classrooms encourage 'discursive knowers'.

7. We should develop curricula which encourage children to think about and see the world as, for example, poets, painters, geographers, scientists, mathematicians, and historians, to explore, represent and understand their worlds and consider how others have done the same.

8. We need better metaphors for classroom life than the industrial production line; such as the poet's study, the artist's studio and the scientist's laboratory.

9. Changing the way we understand and see the world changes us as people, and so changes our identities.

CHAPTER 2

Promoting Thinking Skills Through Talk

Current Concerns

In the course of my work I visit many schools, and speak with and listen to the views of many teachers. I often find myself extolling the virtues of discussion as an approach to learning, but my enthusiasm is always met with the same concern: children these days come to school with impoverished experiences of talk, and many are unable to participate in even the simplest conversation. That teachers have such perceptions was confirmed in a 2003 Basic Skills Agency poll in the UK, in which half of the teachers asked said children were starting school unable to speak audibly, be understood by others, respond to simple instructions, recognize their own names, or even count to five. Another report from Office for Standards in Education (Ofsted) school inspectors in the same year claimed that too many children beginning school lacked basic social skills. Her Majesty's Chief Inspector, David Bell, said the behavioural and verbal skills of children starting school were at an all-time low, adding, 'some five-year-olds cannot even speak properly when they start school'.

Many reasons have been offered for this state of affairs: families spend too much time watching television and this excludes conversations between children, parents and other siblings; the popularity of playing computer games has increased the amount of free time youngsters spend playing alone; and current social trends mean that there are fewer opportunities for family conversations – for example, with some parents working increasingly longer hours and with the ending of institutions such as talk around the dining table. To this list might be added a lack of talking ability on the part of a number of adult parents and carers, which can only add to the problem.

Whatever the reasons, the conclusions are the same: children do not get enough experiences of people talking in ways which promote learning. Nevertheless, some opportunities for informal communication have increased. Consider the use of new technologies such as mobile phones, email and chat rooms – might not these simply be taking the place of traditional conversations? Maybe it is not that children communicate less; they just do so in different ways, not all of them involving talk and face-to-face contact. Perhaps the viewpoints expressed by teachers are more the biases of an older generation than areas for true concern. On the other hand, maybe we are in danger of losing a quality in communication which new technologies cannot replace; a quality which is essential to support learning. I return to this consideration later in the chapter.

These problems are compounded by reduced opportunities for talk in primary classrooms, as confirmed by a study across five countries carried out by Robin Alexander in 2001. Talk is increasingly being squeezed out of a busy, fast-moving, crowded curriculum, in favour of listening. Further, teachers' talk with children tends to focus on checking they know what to do, and it has been claimed that on average pupils can only expect 1 minute 23 seconds of individual attention from their teacher per hour plus an additional 54 seconds per hour as part of a group.

When I started teaching, activities such as 'show and tell' were a part of everyday classroom routine. Each day children would bring in things they wanted to show and talk about, and would take turns to do so whilst the other children were encouraged to be 'good listeners'. In some classrooms similar opportunities still prevail: I recently read an article about a classroom in which each week a different child gets to take a toy dog home and when the child returns, they tell their classmates a story about the toy's adventure. However, for the most part it would appear that opportunities for talk are diminishing, and in response to concerns about speaking skills such as those raised above, lessons in speaking and listening have been proposed by the Qualifications and Curriculum Authority (QCA) as part of the National Primary Strategy for all primary schools in England. The QCA guidance sets age-appropriate expectations: in a group discussion infants should be able to ask and answer relevant questions and suggest ideas; children in years 3 and 4 should use talk to plan and manage work in groups; and top juniors should be able to plan and manage work with minimum supervision. By setting such expectations, there is a danger that they can become ends in themselves. But we should not lose sight of the aims of this initiative: to improve children's learning and social skills by helping them to talk to each other and in groups. As the QCA suggest:

> language is integral to most learning and oral language in particular has a key role in classroom teaching and learning. Children's creativity, understanding and imagination engaged and fostered by discussion and interaction as, in their daily lives, children use speaking and listening to solve problems, speculate, share ideas, make decisions and reflect on what is important.[7]

In this view speaking and listening are means to ends, and not simply ends in themselves.

This recognition is not new: in 1975 the Bullock Report stressed the importance of talk in learning, stating that all schools need to have a commitment to the speech needs of their pupils, and in the late 1980s and early 1990s the National Oracy Project focused on developing an awareness of the importance of talk in children's learning and improving classroom practice. That further strategies are needed indicates a continued lack of awareness amongst teachers as to why it is good for children to talk (see the Reflection Point which follows).

Task 2.1 considers the opportunities which children have to engage in productive talk, and you might like to try it in your class. During the course of a day, note each occasion when the children are engaged in productive talk – that is, talk supporting their learning. Note how many children are involved, who is talking and who is listening, and how long each child's contribution is. Then make comments, perhaps whether it was planned or unplanned, whether children's contributions build on each other, whether they are descriptive or explanatory in nature, whether there are any adults involved in the talk, what their role and influence is, whether they ask questions, if so, what type of questions (for example, open, closed), and how do the children respond. Finally, look at the record as a whole and, in the light of the foregoing discussion, consider any patterns relating to the times when children are engaged in productive talk – is it always the same children, is it generally planned for or spontaneous, what is the nature of the talk and how do adults affect its quality? If you are able to do the audit on a few occasions, or compare your audit with those of colleagues, you might be able to explore further issues such as whether particular subjects seem to offer more opportunities than others.

Task 2.1 Auditing children's talk

During the course of a day note each occasion when children are engaged in productive talk — that is, talk supporting their learning — in the table below. Comments might include whether:

■ it was planned or unplanned;

■ children's contributions built on each other;

■ comments were organizational, descriptive or explanatory in nature;

■ adults were involved.

Finally look at the record as a whole and consider any issues it raises and their implications.

Context of the dialogue, subject/lesson/ time it occured	Number of participants, role of participants and time engaged in dialogue	Comments

Using Thinking Skills in the Primary Classroom © Kelly, 2005

Reflection Point

Why Is It Good To Talk?

What is so important about talk anyway? Does talk matter? Many leading educational thinkers such as Jerome Bruner believe that it matters a great deal. Citing the ideas of the Russian theorist, Lev Vygotsky, social constructivists like Bruner posit a central role for talking in learning: making sense and developing understanding are essentially social processes which take place through talk. The National Oracy Project identified a whole range of ways in which participation with others in activities involving discussion can improve learning: it supports learners in constructing new meanings and understandings as they explore them in words; it allows learners to test out and criticize claims and different points of view as they speak and listen to others; and, most importantly from our perspective on thinking, talk provides raw material for learners' own later private reflective thoughts, because for Vygotsky, thought is an internal, personal dialogue.

However, according to surveys of practice, much of the current emphasis in classrooms is on listening. Further, professional documentation relating to discussion tends to focus on the role of the speaker. But if we think of discourse (and by discourse I mean socially shared talk) as the basis for thinking, then speaking and listening cannot be seen as separate acts: they are closely linked. Dialogue depends on active listening and empathetic speaking if it is to avoid becoming a monologue. Speaking is a complex process: we must listen to and interpret the contributions of others, both in terms of what they are saying and what we feel about what they are saying; then we must relate what has been said and our own stance to the topic of conversation, bringing in our own experiences and anything else we consider to be relevant: and, finally, we must think of something to say which will fit into the conversation and move it forward towards a new understanding of the topic of discussion. In the latter, our contributions might extend, question or clarify what others have said. It is worth observing that, for the discussions to flow, this complex process must happen almost instantaneously.

What we say acts as the basis for others to go through this same process. Interestingly, we can say more than we realize, and through coming to understand what is meant by what has been said, we develop cognitive skills. I wonder how many of us have experienced this whilst teaching: suddenly realizing another significance to something we have said whilst working with a group of children. Speaking is therefore immensely important because it is not just a tool for communicating your ideas to others; it is also a process for changing your ideas and understandings with others.

What We Want and What We Get!

It is interesting to compare the kind of conversations which occur in classrooms with those occurring outside schools. One of the most powerful learning conversations is that between a mother and her child. This is often initiated by the child, and the adult responds in a way which is tailored to the child's needs: it is at the right level, the right speed and gives supportive examples which take into account the child's experiences. Such responses are usually followed by the child exploring what has been said with further questions.

Despite their effectiveness in promoting learning, it would be very difficult to mirror such features in the conversations which teachers and children have in classrooms. However, children's natural conversation with their peers is often as supportive, and can be used to improve learning. Children will agree with and support each other, restate and clarify what others have said, and occasionally challenge. Further, such conversations are often relaxed and unthreatening, allowing children to offer tentative ideas as well as quite personal accounts based on experience, and helping them to make links. Meaning is explored, elaborated and tested out during such discussions, and the explanations which children provide for each other often fit individual needs and offer more appropriate examples than teacher explanations. The act of explaining to others is extremely effective in promoting learning: children can learn by teaching. To explain we must clarify, organize and sometimes reorganize our ideas. If further explanation is required we must then approach things from a different angle. Thus, giving explanations is positively related to achievement.

Unfortunately however, when teachers attempt to join in or engage in such conversations, they often have a negative influence. Children's contributions are reduced, and the talk flows less easily. The children look to the teacher to take the lead, and the teacher usually is happy to respond and take over. Of course, this is because conversations between children have a much more even level of status between participants: all are willing and comfortable to join in on relatively equal terms. When the teacher comes along the children are happy to, indeed expect to, be led by their expertise. They expect to be told what to do.

For the most part, communication in schools is tightly controlled: teachers like ordered classrooms and lessons, and so do children. They are also under tremendous pressure to get through the prescribed curriculum, and this urgency can lead teachers to move discussions towards helping children learn particular things. Of course, children see teachers as the source of their learning, and so accept their teachers' use of questions to control conversations and to steer them in one direction or another. It is therefore not surprising that classroom dialogue is often predictable and routine, with the teacher asking a question, one child responding and the teacher acknowledging the answer as either correct or incorrect. On the few occasions where children are allowed to speak for an extended time, such as when describing something that has happened, the other children grow rapidly bored listening to long rambling contributions. This was often the case during the 'show and tell' activity already mentioned.

All the above suggests that a good place to begin considering how speaking and listening might contribute to children's thinking about learning is in collaborative group work. In the introductory chapter we met the notion that workplaces are increasingly adopting self-directed teams because of the advantages they bestow in terms of responsiveness and flexibility, and because they promote an internal drive towards improvement. However, group work has not been so eagerly adopted in schools: surveys consistently report that, although children are often grouped according to ability for work in English and mathematics, most children sitting in groups work individually. Nevertheless there is substantial evidence that group work in which children share an activity increases achievement, for many of the reasons explored above. Indeed, it is interesting to note that collaborative groups of children tend to spend significantly more time on task than those working individually.

Returning to the notion, introduced earlier, in the Reflection Point, that thinking is an internalized personal dialogue based on our experiences of real discussions and conversations, it is therefore important to engage children in dialogues which reflect the kind of thinking we want them to employ, that is, thinking which: requires them to justify their positions taken on particular issues; enables them to see things from a range of perspectives and considers a range of world views; allows them to construct and explore new meanings and understandings; and engages with and uses big ideas and theoretical models to help explain. The remainder of this chapter explores how we can create opportunities for such productive talk; talk which engages children's thinking skills with their learning.

The Problem with Questions

Suggestions for good practice in developing children's speaking and listening often focus on the effective use of teacher questions. However, as I have already suggested, communication in schools is often tightly controlled with children accepting their teachers' use of questions to steer discussions in one direction or another. To what extent did you identify any of these features in your own practice in Task 2.1?

How might we move away from the predictable and routine responses that such an arrangement provokes from children, and how might we engage the learning of more than one child at a time? Indeed, the kind of thinking we want children to employ, justifying their positions; considering alternative perspectives; constructing and exploring new meanings and understandings; and engaging with big ideas; simply is not going to happen in a climate of overbearing control by the teacher. Without losing the value of sensitive questioning, we must reject the 'chief questioner' role for the teacher, and adopt one which is more helpful in promoting productive talk.

Both these roles are elaborated in the approaches that follow. To successfully adopt either role, teachers need a good level of subject-matter knowledge and an understanding of appropriate models for concepts, theories and big ideas, so as to allow them to provide a degree of expertise and introduce appropriate vocabulary.

Now try Task 2.2. Consider a particular topic which you are working on with your children at the moment. Identify a range of different types of questions, from the focused and closed to those which are open-ended. Finally, think of a group of statements rather than questions which you could say in a conversational way to children. When you have the opportunity, ask these questions as part of your normal activities in class and record children's responses. Consider whether the style of question or statement influences the manner in which the children respond: do narrower questions lead to narrower responses? Do children offer more varied ideas when questions are open and teachers engage in conversations with children?

Good Practice Point

Encouraging Conversations

As an alternative to leading children's talk using questioning, try engaging in conversations with children. You might begin with a statement, for example:

Teacher: I once went on holiday to Greece.

Child 1: We went there last year.

Teacher: I flew from Bristol Airport

Child 2: I've never been on a plane – my mum's scared of flying.

Teacher: What about you? Are you scared?

The trick is to carefully combine statements and questions to allow children to explore an area of interest far more profitably than could take place through teacher questioning. The conversation above is developing into a dialogue in which all members reveal things about themselves and all can ask questions when they want to explore something further.

Task 2.2 Teacher questions

Consider a particular topic which you are working on with your children at the moment. Write down a list of questions which include some which are very focused and closed, some which are more open-ended and, finally, some statements rather than questions which the children could discuss. Now find an opportunity to ask these questions as part of your normal activities in class, recording children's responses. What do you notice as you reduce the control which you exert over these conversations?

Questions	Children's responses
Closed and focused	
Open ended	
Opening statements	

Basic Training

The approaches which follow, which I will refer to collectively as 'learning conversations', require a certain basic competence on the part of the children involved for them to work. I have assumed here that children can express themselves meaningfully through talk and are willing to do so in groups. There is plenty of advice available elsewhere for developing these and this book is not the place for a discussion of approaches to teaching speaking and listening at the level of basic communication.

Good Practice Point

Establishing Ground Rules

There are a number of ground rules which need to be established with children in relation to learning conversations. Rules to stop interruptions of all those involved in group work, whether adults or children, should be negotiated first. Thus children needing help might be encouraged to take greater responsibility for their learning by seeking support elsewhere, or by doing alternative work until support is available.

Learning conversations should be democratic: everyone has the right to a say, and for their contribution to be valued. This means that participants in learning conversations should:

- listen attentively to the contributions of others without interrupting;

- speak to each other, looking at the person to whom they are responding;

- take turns and allow everyone an equal opportunity to speak;

- be sensitive to each others' needs;

- try to see things from other people's points of view, even if they disagree with their position;

- give reasons for their views;

- be prepared to change their viewpoint in the light of new information, and accept others doing the same.

Further, children should understand that it is disrespectful to others if they monopolize the talk or if they ridicule or are unkind about others or their views. Of course, it is often most effective when the children are allowed to come up with rules such as these themselves: with prompting they can be encouraged to address the key areas. A good place to develop these together with a regard for democratic ways of working is the school council.

Once ground rules have been established, children's awareness of further, more complex skills, including:

- active engagement;

- probing and question raising;

- helping others through talk;

- clarity and openness;

- a willingness to take risks;

- an awareness of the importance of inner speech;

can be raised and specific group work tools and techniques such as brainstorming can be taught. The extent of these skills is briefly illustrated below, and examples of prompts which can be used to promote these skills are provided in Figure 2.1.

Skill	Prompts
Active engagement	What are the main features of the idea? How does the viewpoint being offered address the area being considered? Does the viewpoint 'hang together' or makes sense? How does it link to my ideas or those of other members of the group? Can I visualize this idea? Do I want to change my idea in the light of this new idea?
Probing and question raising	What are the consequences of what you have said? What might your ideas lead to? Does this apply to all situations? Are there any contradictions? Is this the best approach? What are its strengths and weaknesses?
Helping others	What might we look at first, next? How can we go about this? Has everyone had an opportunity to contribute? Shall we take a vote? What does each of us think about this?
Clarity and openness	Can you justify what you have said? What do you mean by that? Can you explain again in a different way? Can you provide me with an example of that? Can you tell me more about that?

Figure 2.1 Prompts for encouraging complex conversation skills

Active Engagement

When listening to viewpoints and ideas, children should try to focus on understanding the idea being put forward, perhaps by visualizing it. This 'intention to understand' can be facilitated by considering how the viewpoint being offered addresses the area being considered, whether the viewpoint 'hangs together' or makes sense and how it links to their own ideas or those offered by other members of the group. These might be provided initially as a series of prompts, and the teacher might provide examples of how they might respond to these.

Probing and Question-Raising

In the process of active listening the child might need clarification of, or further elaboration on, the speaker's views. So, they might like the speaker to put it in another way or provide an example; they might want the speaker to address an apparent inconsistency in what they have said; or they might like to explore the consequences or implications of a proposal or idea.

Helping Others Through Talk

Conversations sometimes need encouragement to get going. Patience and inclusive phrases and actions are important. This might include asking for the opinion of a reticent group member or suggesting a way to begin considering an area.

Clarity and Openness in Expression

It is important for children to consider the rest of their group, by trying to be clear in what they say both vocally and in terms of the meanings they are trying to convey. In the latter, children should be encouraged to be open and honest about their ideas.

A Willingness to Take Risks

Part of making learning conversations exciting and creative involves speakers taking risks in what they offer to the group for consideration. Of course, this is hard to encourage, and many factors inhibit risk-taking, including personal levels of confidence and perceptions of identity, academic levels of understanding and skill in communication, and social pressures from peers and the teacher. Risk-taking is only possible if the classroom climate addresses all of these – most importantly, by valuing everyone's contributions and accepting diversity in opinion.

An Awareness of Inner Speech

Of course, the rational for this work is that the conversations in which children engage provide a model for their own future 'inner speech' or thinking. Therefore, when we talk of active listening and thinking about what had been said, we are reliant on the learner being able to have an internal dialogue to deliberate the contributions of others and to rehear their own contributions. Raising an awareness of this inner dialogue can support learners in adopting in their own thinking the ideas and approaches which they have heard used in discussion.

Through the process of engaging in learning conversations, children can be supported in developing their ability to articulate a point of view and to engage in discussion and reasoning. After finishing tasks they can be helped to reflect on how the group has worked, monitoring group processes for skills such as conciseness, listening, reflecting, and allowing all members to contribute, and monitoring their own behaviour in groups.

Good Practice Point

Prompting Complex Communication Skills

It is important that children become familiar with the skills and prompts in Figure 2.1. After they have been introduced to the children they should be revisited regularly: perhaps this list of communication skills and prompts could be displayed and referred to at the start of each discussion, and discussions could be evaluated once they have ended using the same prompts.

Some schools introduce the skills and prompts progressively from year 3 onwards, rewriting them in age-appropriate language and often beginning with 'helping others'. Other schools plan to look at all the skills each year, but focus on each one separately at different times during the year.

Approaches to Using Dialogue for Thinking About Learning

I have suggested that it is important to engage children in dialogues which reflect the kind of thinking we want them to employ, that is, thinking in which they have to justify positions taken on particular issues and which helps them see things from a range of perspectives and considers a range of world views, allows them to construct and explore new meanings and understandings, and engages with and uses big ideas and theoretical models to help provide explanations. Thus it is important to get children talking with each other and with adults, sharing knowledge, skills and understandings in their conversations, and adopting ways of working (such as those involved in drafting a story or carrying out a scientific investigation) which allow them to get things done and build new knowledge. Approaches to learning conversations include:

- one-to-one conferences with teachers (consideration of this is left until the next chapter);

- collaborative group work;

- dialogical enquiry;

- authentic activity (consideration of this is left until Chapter 4).

The characteristics of these different types of learning conversation is outlined in Figure 2.2.

Type	Organization	Purpose
Conference	One to one, child with teacher, child's reflections facilitated by teacher	Centres on the importance of reflection, and aims to develop in children critically reflective thinking. Allows learners to develop narrative coherence in their knowledge.
Collaborative group work	Mixed ability, gender balanced group of four children, working together collaboratively to achieve a shared goal	The group of children work together to produce a tangible outcome, be it a product (such as a poem) or a solution (such as an answer to problems).
Dialogical enquiry	Pair, small group or whole-class discussions sometimes involving the teacher and sometimes not	This allows learners, through language and sometimes supported by written notes and prompts, to jointly engage in using and creating knowledge. In this they will justify their position, consider a range of perspectives and ideas, and develop new meanings and understandings.
Authentic activity	Groups of children supported by experts	Children engage in the purposeful activities of particular communities of practice, supported by experts. So, for science, children work as scientists, engaging in an enquiry: - for which the answer is not already known; - which involves children in using the key ideas and tools of science; - which is purposeful, and aim to meet such purposes; - which is intelligible to those involved; - which involves a partnership with others who have an interest or expertise in the object or process of enquiry.

Figure 2.2 Characteristics of different types of learning conversation

Children also need to be led towards the thinking of experts (including teachers). Here the experts must expose their thinking through talk, allowing learners to see how they use their knowledge, skills and understandings, and the processes in which they engage to, for example, solve a problem. Then they might support the child in copying their expert model, gradually reducing the support until the child can do it alone. A useful approach here is reciprocal teaching, where the child takes on the role of teacher in the group. These are all central features of authentic enquiry which is considered fully in Chapter 4. Metacognitive evaluation approaches (that is, approaches to reflecting on and controlling your own learning) are also important here and can be taught in a similar way. These are considered in the next chapter. However in the remainder of this chapter I focus on collaborative group work and dialogical enquiry

Collaborative Group Work

When we think of joint activities we focus on the group as a community that works towards shared goals; the achievement of these goals depends on collaboration. In this sense the group is more than the sum of its individual members. Every activity is unique, because it depends on the collaborative efforts of particular individuals, at a particular time, in a particular place using particular mental and physical resources. The learning outcomes of activity cannot be completely known or prescribed in advance. Such activities can allow individuals to work beyond their individual capabilities, and be creative in striving for novel solutions.

Good Practice Point

Organizing Collaborative Group Work

Research has suggested that the ideal size for groups engaging in collaborative work is four – pairs are too small for generating lots of ideas, threes tend to form a pair and exclude the third member, and groups bigger than four become harder for the children to manage so it is less likely that everyone will be fully included. Similarly mixed gender and mixed ability groups tend to be more inclusive, focused and generate the widest range of viewpoints and ideas.

There are two basic forms of task organization for collaborative work: 'jigsaw' and 'group investigation'. The former requires each group member to complete a sub-task which contributes to the whole group completing the assigned task. This might be the production of a picture, diagram or piece of writing about, say, Roman villas for a group display on that topic. In the second, all in the group work together on the same task, with each member of the group being assigned a different role. So the children might create a small dramatic episode portraying life in a Roman villa. Each child would play a different character and, in addition, one child might take on the role of director.

The academic and social demands of tasks like these are, of course, closely linked, but must be considered carefully if they are to match the capabilities and needs of the group. So, in providing tasks such as investigating, using as many available sources as possible, why a Roman city like Exeter was situated where it was, the academic demands include whether the children understand the reasons why a settlement might develop in a particular place – meeting transport, food, defence and other needs – and the social demands include whether the children can organize themselves to access the relevant information together, and make decisions of relevance, their relative importance and how to present their final ideas. An example of a completed collaborative group-work planning document is provided in Figure 2.3, which includes notes on the roles of individual group members and the sub-tasks they are required to complete.

Shared goal:	To explore why less children are having school dinners at our school now than this time last year, and recommend ways of halting this decline.				
Date:	Monday 5th March; Tuesday 6th March	**Time:**	1:30-2:30; 2:00-3:15	**Year:**	6

Learning demands	
Academic	**Social**
Identifying information required; Planning how to gain that information; Designing interviews, survey questionnaires, etc; Statistical data analysis, and interview analysis; Bringing information together, drawing conclusions	Organizing themselves to access the relevant information together; Showing clarity and sensitivity whilst interviewing; Making decisions of relevance, relative importance and how to present their final ideas

Name	**Allocated role or sub-task**
Whole group with teacher support	Identifying information required and plan how to gain that information – if not raised by group, suggest use of 'office data' to identify children for interviews, use of surveys for other children and interview other key individuals
Callum Barnard and Melissa Breer	Look at one class and check with the school administrator which children who regularly had school meals last year don't do so now; Design an interview questionnaire for those children; Interview them
Josie Hayles and David James	Design a survey for children in 3 classes to complete; Distribute and collect survey; Interview meal time assistants about their views
Whole group	Consider all data, write a joint report of why this might be and anything relevant, making suggestions for action
Additional support	**Role**
Mrs Sanderson (Administrative Assistant)	Help children find out who regularly had school meals last year but don't do so now

Figure 2.3 Example of a collaborative group-work task planning document

Group tasks are most effective when children need to share their knowledge, skills and understandings to a common end through some form of problem-solving or open-ended task with one correct solution from many alternatives. In their activity, children's talk will centre initially on their actions, but should be moved towards their understandings. I address this further in the next section.

Task 2.3 is about planning a collaborative group-work activity in the context of your class and their current areas of learning. Consider the suggestions above and, perhaps, the Lesson Ideas below to make your plan. Then observe the children engaged in the activity and talk to them after they have completed the task. You might like to consider the extent to which each child was on task and engaged during the task, how the work was distributed amongst the group, whether the entire group contributed equally, whether the group was successful in meeting their shared goal and, finally, whether, once they had completed the task, they felt the task had helped them.

Task 2.3 Collaborative group work

Use the text and the grid below to plan a collaborative group-work activity. Observe the children engaged in the activity and talk to them after they have completed the task. To what extent do you feel that each child was on task and engaged during the task? How was the work distributed and did the entire group contribute equally? Were they successful in meeting their shared goal? After they had completed the task, how did they feel the task had helped them?

	Collaborative group-work task planning document				
Shared goal:					
Date:		**Time:**		**Year:**	
	Learning demands				
	Academic		Social		
	Name	Allocated role or sub-task			
	Additional support	Role			

Using Thinking Skills in the Primary Classroom © Kelly, 2005

Lesson Ideas (with a suggested Thinking Skills emphasis): Collaborative Groups

A group might work together on a 'jigsaw task' to produce a leaflet welcoming newcomers and informing them about the school. Each child might survey a different group of children from across the school to find out what information newcomers would need and benefit from. Particular attention would be paid to the experiences of any newcomers to the school. Then the group would make decisions together about which areas to address, in what format, and so on. Each child could then be allocated the task of developing an aspect of the leaflet, with these being finally brought together for the finished document. (*Possible Thinking Skills Emphasis: decision-making*)

In mathematics a group might work together on a 'group-task' triangular numbers problem: having been introduced to the sequence of triangular numbers they could be set the challenge of finding the 10th and 100th triangular numbers by the simplest method and then showing that their answer is correct. (*Possible Thinking Skills Emphasis: searching for meaning*)

Dialogical Enquiry

Dialogical enquiries are discussions in which learners, through language and sometimes supported by written notes and prompts, jointly engage in using and creating knowledge. Participants need to be committed to:

- working towards a common understanding for all;
- asking questions and suggesting ideas relating to the evidence on which proposals are based;
- looking at issues and problems from as many different perspectives as possible;
- challenging ideas and perspectives in the light of contradictions and evidence so as to move the discussion forwards.

Such enquiries may follow or precede collaborative group-work activities. Obviously not necessarily separate or exclusive, and may both form part of one activity. Using this link can help children who are new to dialogical enquiries:

- They can begin by sharing information about and describing how they did the activity, and describing their first-hand experiences of the collaborative group work activity.
- They can compare their experiences and findings – looking at similarities and differences between these.
- They can begin to work towards a joint understanding of the problem, process of enquiry, findings and implications. This involves knowledge-building.

Thus in the collaborative group-work example given in Figure 2.3, the group will engage in such a dialogical enquiry at the end of their data-collecting activities, considering issues of school-meal uptake. Here the dialogue is aimed at finding an answer to the question or a solution to the problem from which the activity has arisen. However they might then engage in a further dialogical enquiry with other groups in the class engaged in similar data collecting and analysis activities within their class, but this time focusing on the wider issues in data collection and analysis.

Of course not all dialogical enquiries will arise from collaborative group-work activities. Thus a group of learners might consider the ethical dilemmas surrounding euthanasia. First, they read together two articles outlining the case for and against. They then take it in turn to state their position and why, and respond to the positions adopted by other members of the group. Later they are able to change their position or add to it, until the group has established either a common position on which it can agree or a number of alternatives which encapsulate the main areas of difference within the group.

Good Practice Point

Using Text in Dialogical Enquiry

The problem with any conversation or discussion is that once it is over the participants are left with no record of it other than what they remember. However, by including writing in dialogical enquiries we can not only record some aspect of the discourse, but also create far more powerful knowledge-building situations.

Many believe that writing simply records knowledge and ideas. Children think of an idea, an answer, a story, an explanation and then they write it. But those with greater experience of writing know that this simple picture does not fully account for what is going on. Writing actually shapes our thinking. Thus, as I write at my computer I reread what I have written and change it – perhaps in the reading I realize that the phrase I have written means more than I intended it to, perhaps I am forging links between ideas or the process of reading is helping me generate new ideas. Whatever is happening, I am engaged in a discourse with my writing, and in doing so am changing it as it is changing me: writing is a knowledge-transforming activity.

Lesson Ideas (with a suggested Thinking Skills Emphasis): Dialogical Enquiry

Dialogical enquiries take the notion of one person having an internal dialogue with a text, and extend it to many people having a shared dialogue with both the text and each other. Thus activities such as book clubs or reading circles are important, where children can discuss their reading and produce new books together. Similarly writing conferences, in which writers discuss their writing with their peers, are extremely valuable. Of course, having such shared dialogues about texts will improve participants' ability to engage in such dialogues alone. (*Possible Thinking Skills Emphasis: being creative*)

This notion of a shared dialogue about a text fits in well with assessment approaches which we consider in the next chapter, including conferencing, negotiated feedback and peer assessment. (*Possible Thinking Skills Emphasis: making critical judgements*)

Other opportunities exist in developing home–school learning partnerships in children's work. Thus, in one example, parents of a particular group of young children read the same book with their children at home one evening. During the shared reading, parents wrote down the children's responses to the stories on Post-it notes and fixed them to the relevant pages. Next day these notes became the starting points for discussion between the teacher and the group. (*Possible Thinking Skills Emphasis: searching for meaning*)

With older children each child in a group reading the same book together might individually write a prediction of the next stage of the story. This writing might provide the starting point for a group discussion about the evidence for each prediction, likelihood and plausibility of each prediction and the groups preferred outcome. Such a discussion could equally be based on individual group members writing initially from the perspective of one of the characters of the story and providing that character's point of view. The discussion could then consider the story from this variety of perspectives. (*Possible Thinking Skills Emphasis: being creative*)

Other useful textual starting points which can be considered individually or in small groups before bringing to a larger group include: ideas of questions raised at the start of a new unit of work which the children would like to explore; designs and plans of action for technological work, investigative work and problem-solving activities; interpretations of data in mathematics, science or geography; texts on, for example, historical events providing differing perspectives; and many more. (*Possible Thinking Skills Emphasis: problem-solving*)

In terms of interpretation of data, such discursive enquiries are important because they can link the process of enquiry to the big ideas of the subject. So, for example, in science following an investigation of the conditions in which plants grow best, rather than children simply describing the conditions which are most favourable to healthy plant growth, the discussion can focus on ideas about why this might be the case. Perhaps the children's text of the data collected can be compared in their discussion to other writing they have done which has attempted to explain findings. (*Possible Thinking Skills Emphasis: being creative*)

Good Practice Point

Time to Reflect

Following their involvement in learning conversations, children also need times to reflect, to be quiet and to engage in activities designed to make use of their expanding repertoire of inner dialogues.

Reflection Point

Distant Conversations

Earlier I raised the issue of whether communication via new technologies is the same as face-to-face communication. Face-to-face conversations can involve many people, with non-participants thinking and listening, whilst others are talking. The latter also occurs in online communities, but the issue of similarity begs some questions. For example, is reading a contribution to an online community and then writing a response the same as listening and speaking in a traditional conversation? Consider the role of other non-verbal cues. Although mobile phones and video conferencing try to reduce the physical 'distance' between participants, they cannot entirely mimic direct conversation because they retain a barrier to talk by denying full access to expression and non-verbal cues.

But even if we accept and compensate for the limitation or absence of the non-verbal, written discourse in online communities is altogether different to talk. There may be less risk-taking in written discourse, because of the commitment which a writer makes to a contribution when writing it down – with the possibility that it will be read by others. Contributions in conversations can be suggested tentatively, and withdrawn quickly if they are met with disapproval: steps can be taken to ensure that no 'damage is done', and there is no record other than in the memory of the person you're talking to.

Further, talk involves speech without considered reflection, whereas typed dialogue lacks the immediacy of reply. Written contributions are transformed by the writer in drafting contributions before the process of discourse, but speech is more likely to be transformed in the process of discourse. Thus drafted writing is often clearer and slicker, including hedging phrases using words such as 'might' and 'perhaps', and lacks the bold assertions and impassioned contributions of spontaneous talk. A further online consequence of this is the reduced opportunity for creative misinterpretation which can take the conversational discourse in unexpected directions.

All these things mean that online discourses are likely to be qualitatively different from face-to-face ones. Thus my own view is that, although online discourses can make great contributions to learning, they will never replace face-to-face work because of these differences. I am sure that this is an area which deserves and will receive much future attention from educationalists.

Talking Classrooms

Discourse is a vital tool in engaging and using children's thinking skills in the classroom. It helps children to use their learning and to create new ideas. In addition it models for children how they can use their thinking skills in their own inner dialogue. Thus it is essential that we provide opportunities for productive talk if we want to develop thinking classrooms.

Key Points

1. Making sense and developing understanding are social processes which take place through talk. Thought is an internal, personal dialogue which is modelled on the external dialogues in which we engage.

2. Children accept their teachers' use of questions to steer discussions in one direction or another:

   (a) The teacher can act as a model of participation and expertise, scaffolding children's own participation.

   (b) The teacher can act as a facilitator of discussions.

3. Learning conversations provide a structure and context for these teacher roles.

4. Participants in learning conversations should:

   (a) listen attentively to the contributions of others without interrupting;

   (b) speak to each other, looking at the person to whom they are responding;

   (c) take turns and allow everyone an equal opportunity to speak;

   (d) be sensitive to each others needs;

   (e) try to see things from other people's points of view, even if they disagree with their position;

(f) give reasons for their views;

(g) be prepared to change their viewpoint in the light of new information, and accept others doing the same.

5. Children's engagement in learning conversations can be improved if their awareness of the following complex skills is raised:

(a) active engagement;

(b) probing and question-raising;

(c) helping others through talk;

(d) clarity and openness;

(e) a willingness to take risks;

(f) an awareness of the importance of inner speech.

6. Approaches to learning conversations include:

(a) one-to-one conferences with teachers (considered in the next chapter);

(b) collaborative group work;

(c) dialogical enquiry;

(d) authentic activity (considered in Chapter 4).

7. Collaborative group work works best with mixed ability, gender-balanced groups of about four children.

8. Dialogical enquiries can involve pairs, small group or whole-class discussions sometimes involving the teacher. They allow learners to jointly engage in using and creating knowledge.

9. By including writing in dialogical enquiries we can not only record some aspect of the discourse, but also create far more powerful knowledge-building situations.

10. Online discourses are likely to be qualitatively different from face-to-face ones and it is unlikely that they will ever replace face-to-face work.

Promoting Thinking Skills Through Assessment

The Social Nature of Assessment

As human beings we like to be valued and recognized by others, especially if we value them. Indeed, we need such affirmations. We are deeply social, and what counts is how we see ourselves and how we think others see us. We choose friends who have similar interests, dispositions and who make us feel good about ourselves: they are interested and they make us feel worthwhile. In turn they interest us, and we make them feel of worth. Through subtle behaviours we affirm each other, and the pain is great when such relationships break down. Classrooms are built on relationships. We learn socially by participating in joint activities, in which learning is sustained through an emotional involvement.

The power of this need for approval is immense. Consider the lengths youngsters will go to gain the affirmation of their peers. And consider the impact which criticism can have on people's lives, especially when the individual concerned sees the criticism of their performance as being a criticism of them as a person.

When we look at assessment in this light, it is little wonder that it has such an influence on our children. By providing approval and affirmation, assessment can actually change our lives and make us who we become: it can shape us as people and give us confidence to act positively in the world.

Such a view recognizes that assessment is so much a social process. But it also recognizes the power assessment can have in shaping our interests and focusing our efforts. This drive for approval means that we will strive to meet the requirements of those things which we think 'count' amongst those around us. Thus in schools, many children strive to meet the assessment requirements of their classrooms and seek the approval of their teachers and the respect of their peers. Thus, for assessment to enable us to shape rounded and thoughtful individuals it should recognize each child's full range of abilities, encompassing those areas of learning which help make us what we are, such as our capacity to form positive relationships, our abilities to see things from various perspectives, and our vast range of potentials. In this we should develop forms of assessment which assess the knowledge, skills and attitudinal objectives which we value most in the curriculum: for instance, where co-operative skills and attitudes are prioritized, these must also be the focus for assessment. Further, assessment should acknowledge the complexity of each individual by considering their abilities and areas of difficulty in many ways and from many perspectives.

But assessment must not just be a source of external approval: it should support the development of children's internal drives to make meaning and succeed. It should nurture a love of learning for its own sake, and encourage learners to enter their learning with an intention to understand. To do this, children must be regarded first and foremost as 'partners in' rather than 'subjects of' assessment processes. Further, if we are to succeed we need to nurture children's development in a humane way: learners have a right to expect their dignity to be fully respected and every child has the right to be given a voice in matters concerning them.

Of course, we can do these things within the cosy confines of the classroom, but we have little influence on children's lives beyond school. However, if we are to reach out to the world, we must assess in meaningful, social contexts where assessment is an integral part of the activities of children and contributes to their success in achieving the desired outcomes of the activity. Much classroom activity can be individual and divorced from life outside school. However, environments most helpful to deep learning encourage co-operation and interaction with everyday and community concerns and experiences. Assessment which focuses on problem-solving, thematic enquiries and the like in co-operative contexts is therefore central to supporting the development of deep and transferable understandings in learners.

If learning is a journey, then assessment is like keeping a diary on that journey. We might ask what kind of relationship people should have with these diaries. For some the diary is simply a means of recording events. But many people have a far more positive and powerful relationship with their diaries ('Dear Diary … '), it is honest but understanding, critical but forward looking, reflective and transformational. This latter relationship is that which I believe children should have with assessment in their classrooms.

Principles for Promoting Thinking Skills Through Assessment

So, on the basis of the preceding discussion, there are a number of principles we can adopt for assessment which promotes the use of thinking skills.

1. For assessment to promote rounded and thoughtful individuals whose learning reaches out from the classroom to engage with the world:

    (a) teachers should make assessments which relate to underpinning curricular values, making these public, and not simply concentrate on what is easiest to assess. This will require teachers to develop new methods to assess attitudes, beliefs, understandings and skills;

    (b) teachers sometimes should assess the same knowledge in a variety of contexts, both schooling and other, and over a period of time, recognizing that context and time are issues. Such assessments can be collected in portfolios, providing both a richer assessment profile than a series of single assessment 'snapshots' and a basis for assessment dialogues between children and others;

(c) teachers should ensure that they use a variety of observational, oral, discursive and written approaches, including testing, to make both formative (offering guidance on how best to revise the teaching and learning process and on how best to meet the needs of the individual child within that process) and summative (offering a summary assessment of what a child has learnt at a particular point) assessments of learning. Each of these approaches should be recognized by all – children, parents and teachers – as being of equal value;

(d) children, parents and teachers should fully recognize the 'baggage', that is, the assumptions and limitations, that each assessment method brings with it and take these into account when interpreting data;

(e) finally, children, parents and teachers should consider all these approaches and issues when making overall judgements of student performance and school effectiveness in relation to teaching.

2. For assessment to encourage thoughtful approaches and deep engagement then we must:

(a) consider the process of learning and not just the product;

(b) engage in approaches which encourage children to explain and try to understand their reasoning;

(c) discuss problems so that children reveal their ways of thinking.

3. For assessment to promote a love of learning for its own sake, and to encourage learners to enter their learning with an intention to understand, and for assessment to be part of that learning process, and developing metacognitive and reflective approaches:

(a) children should be regarded as partners in the learning process and be involved in the appraisal of their own learning and understanding, having opportunities for extended assessment dialogues (both oral and written) with teachers and peers;

(b) teacher feedback needs to move beyond grading work (in which grades become an end in themselves) to encouraging a deep approach to learning with an understanding intention on the part of the learner. In this, teacher feedback should be dialogic and should promote a learning partnership with the child. This can result in negotiated focuses for student development coupled with agreed support, through a process of target-setting with children;

(e) self-assessment, which grows from feedback, must be modelled and coached with children, and at best engages learners in a metacognitive dialogue which goes beyond 'how did you think you did?' towards considerations such as:

(i) Which areas fit in well with other areas of your learning?

(ii) Where are there inconsistencies?

(iii) Which areas could you explain to another student?

(iv) How do these ideas fit with your experience away from school?

(v) How do these ideas fit or fail to fit with your own sense of yourself?

Such assessments might form part of a learning log, diary or journal;

(d) peer assessment adds a further important perspective and supports learners in positive identity formation. Additionally it allows the child's peers to reflect on their own position whilst contributing towards the child's appraisal;

(e) reporting should be clear, accurate, accessible and informative, attempting to be faithful to the complexity of child attainment and focusing on a learning partnership between the child, parent and teacher.

Do you agree with these principles? To what extent do they apply to your current context? Are there areas you feel you are addressing well and areas you are less sure about? In the following sections I consider how such principles might be adopted in practice.

Promoting Rounded and Thoughtful Individuals

There are times when structured assessment tasks are required to focus on the assessment of specific learning. The approach adopted will depend on what is to be assessed, but it is important that whatever is assessed a variety of approaches are used. So, for assessing the acquisition of knowledge, there are many well-known approaches including using:

- direct questions;

- multiple choice questions;

- sentence completion tasks;

- asking children to write in their own words, explain, and discuss consequences and implications;

- cloze exercises, where text about an area of learning is provided with key words missing. Children have to insert the correct words, which can also be provided in a list, or left entirely to the children to decide on the most appropriate word;

- concept or mental mapping, which can be produced by children prior to or following a particular study.

Similarly the application of knowledge can be assessed through providing problem-solving activities and investigations for children to tackle. However, it is important that these include problems and activities in a variety of contexts.

The assessment approaches listed above will be familiar to most teachers and are treated fully elsewhere, so I do not consider them further here. However, there are other important areas to be addressed when making 'rounded assessments' which are not so well covered, and it is to these that I now turn.

Assessing Attitudes and Beliefs

An area which deserves consideration is children's attitudes and beliefs. How might we assess these? One way is provided in Task 3.1. Try giving the attitudinal survey entitled 'What I think about school' to a group of children, either to be completed individually or in small groups. Following this, look at the children's responses: what do these tell you about their attitudes to school and the usefulness of surveys as a method of assessment?

This is a very simplistic approach, which might be useful in beginning a debate with children about their attitudes and beliefs but which is quite unreliable in assessing those attitudes and beliefs: as with any survey, findings depend on how seriously respondents have taken it, how they have interpreted questions, whether those questions were leading or misleading and how well the survey has covered the key areas. Figure 3.1 provides a categorization of beliefs which can be used in a more sophisticated approach to appraising children's beliefs about learning. Variations on the questions across the top of the taxonomy can be asked of the children, perhaps relating to different subjects and in different ways, and the children's answers categorized. Teacher–student conferences, which we discuss in a later section, provide a good opportunity for this.

Stage	Student focus	What they believe is learnt	How they believe it is learnt	How they believe learning is used
1	Students focus on doing the work without understanding	Students emphasize the need to follow instructions	Students learn by repetition and practice	Learning is used to do more work and to pass tests
2	Students focus on learning to complete the task	Students are a little less dependent, but little flexibility and easily set off course	Students learn by being shown and then practising themselves with coaching	Learning is used to do the things you learn to do – so you can work out how much things cost when shopping using mathematics or write letters to a pen friend using language work
3	Students focus on thinking about the task, on understanding and on solving problems	Students are creative, skilful and show care and pride in their work	Students learn through discussions, group work and individual reflection	Learning is used to help you when you are older and want to get a job
4	Students understand and analyse the task and their learning from it, they use their learning in other areas including investigations and solving problems	Students search for patterns, make generalizations and seek to understand situations	Students learn through enquiry and reflection, and must take responsibility for their own learning	Learning helps you see the world in a different way, like a scientist, a mathematician, a poet or an artist

Figure 3.1 Taxonomy of students' beliefs about learning

Task 3.1 Surveying attitudes

Give the following attitudinal survey about 'What I think about school' to a group of children to complete individually or in small groups.

Then consider:

1. What are the main findings from your analysis of the children's responses? Were there any surprises for you?

2. What is the value of this form of assessment? Do you feel the information it provides is accurate? Could it be improved?

How do you feel about these statements?	Agree	Neutral	Disagree
1. When I get up in the morning, I look forward to going to school.			
2. The children in school are nice to smaller children (about their work).			
3. My teacher usually has time to listen to my questions.			
4. When I am at home, I sometimes think of things to tell my teacher about.			
5. When I am at home, I talk about things I have been doing at school.			
6. I read to someone at home.			
7. I read to myself at home.			
8. I know what sort of work I am good at.			
9. My parents come to school and talk to my teacher.			
10. When I have finished my work at school, I usually know what to do next.			
11. My work is usually boring.			
12. Sometimes my teacher thinks my work is really good.			
13. When I need help, my teacher helps me.			
14. A lot of the work is too easy for me.			
15. When my teacher looks at my work, I feel good.			
16. I get stuck a lot.			
17. When my teacher shows my work to the class, I worry about what people will say afterwards.			
18. I am going to be good at school work when I am older.			
19. What you learn at school is important for you when you are grown up.			

Using Thinking Skills in the Primary Classroom © Kelly, 2005

So, for example, when asked about some mathematical work in his conference with the teacher, Ben said, 'When we first learned to do these I was in Class 4. I just remembered what to do each time and then I'd be able to do all of the sums without thinking about them'. This comment shows Ben is focusing on doing the work by repetition without understanding and learning. These beliefs fall into Stage 1 of the above taxonomy.

Assessing Discursive and Co-operative Skills

A second area deserving consideration for assessment is discursive and co-operative skills. In the next section we will be considering teacher observation as a powerful assessment approach. During the process of assessment the teacher might be looking with a particular focus, and statements such as those in Figure 3.2 can provide a useful basis for categorizing observations relating to how well children speak and listen to each other and how well they work together in groups.

Stage	Evaluative criteria
1	Students are able to participate in group work of different kinds, understanding how to use talk purposefully in pairs and small groups and contribute ideas to whole-class discussions. When working in groups they should be able to take turns, and help to say what they have done.
2	Students can sustain different roles within groups with little intervention from the teacher. They can take the lead and draw ideas together. They can comment on how a task has been managed and reflect on the group's strengths and weaknesses.
3	Students can organize and manage collaborative tasks with minimal supervision. They can negotiate disagreements and ways of overcoming them, suggesting alternative courses of action, clarifying differences and putting ideas to the vote.

Figure 3.2 Taxonomy of students' discursive and co-operative skills

Source: adapted from the National Primary Strategy document QCA (2003) *Speaking and Listening Handbook*. London: QCA.

Assessing Learning Preferences

Finally, learners can benefit enormously from being aware of their own learning preferences. Task 3.2 comprises a questionnaire which can be used to begin this process. Remembering the expressed in relation to attitudinal surveys, this can be a useful starting point for self-evaluation and discussion, again in the context of teacher–student conferences.

Encouraging Thoughtful Approaches and Deep Engagement

Teacher and Pupil Observation

Observation is an important means of assessment because there is an emphasis on the process of learning. It involves:

- looking at the way pupils go about their work and not just the products of their activity;

Task 3.2 Profile your learning preferences

Look at the following survey/questionnaire. How might this help you identify children's preferred learning dispositions? How useful would the information it provides be? What would you need to be cautious of?

What do you learn best?

1. Which of these do you find easiest to remember?

	Hard	OK	Easy
The way to a friends house			
Jokes			
The names of new friends			
Faces of relatives who live far away			
A new word			
Who won each race on last sports day			
How to use the photocopier			
A recipe you heard from a friend			

2. What do you find easiest to understand?

	With effort	Not too much of a problem	Easily
The plot of a story I am reading			
How to use punctuation marks in my writing			
How things work			
How to do mathematical problems			
Coming up with arguments for and against something happening			
Graphs			

3. What are you best at?

	No way!	I can do it if I have to!	I do well at this!
Creative writing			
Talking and giving my own views in discussions			
Resolving conflicts between friends			
Doing something again when I've made a mistake			
Playing instruments and singing			
Taking part in sports			
Working out mathematical problems			
Understanding and explaining how things work			
Painting and drawing			

Using Thinking Skills in the Primary Classroom © Kelly, 2005

- listening to pupils ideas and trying to understand their reasoning;

- discussing problems so that pupils reveal their ways of thinking.

Observation has a number of advantages:

- It is flexible and can be used at any time.

- It does not interfere with normal classroom activities or take up time.

- It can provide information about behaviours of all kinds.

- It can be used repeatedly, giving constant feedback.

- Children are unaware of the process.

- It does not require special equipment or materials.

Opportunities for observation can be negotiated with the children. For example, the teacher might say, 'I am looking to see what you are doing and how you are learning, and will be carrying a red folder when doing this, so you'll know not to disturb me'. The children will pick up quickly what is happening, and often respond well.

When observing, teachers should focus on one group, a pair, or just one child for a short time. Observation should be purposeful, and the teacher should record what is observed. It can be:

- open, that is, non-judgemental, non-specific. Here the observer looks to see what captures the imagination of those being observed;

- focused, by looking at an individual child or at interactions between children in a group. The teacher might consider children's 'on-task' activity, their language usage, or their selection and use of resources, without particular categories to guide their attention. Thus the teacher can identify patterns;

- systematic, where categories are identified beforehand and the observations often focus on timed sampling of behaviour in terms of the prescribed categories.

Good Practice Point

Systematic Observation

The intention with systematic observation is that clear procedures can be followed by observers such that any observer should record a particular event in an identical way to any other. The reason for carrying out the observation is decided upon before the data is collected. This might relate to how the child carries out the task, how they work with others and/or the quality of what is said. The teacher observes the child over a 10–20 minute period, and uses the structured observation sheet to record observations (see Figure 3.3). Every minute the teacher writes down what the child is doing, and what is being said/what they are saying. This is written without interpretation. Following the period of observation the teacher can classify their recorded observations using specific categories and criteria relating to the observation focus. This focus might be in relation to children's discursive and co-operative skills (see Figure 3.2) or their level of thinking using the SOLO taxonomy (see Figure 3.5).

Child's name:	Gender:	Age:	Date and time observed:	
What the child does	**What the child says and what is said to the child**	**Discursive/ co-operative skills**	**Level of thinking**	
1.				
2.				
3.				
4.				
5.				
6.				
7.				
8.				
9.				
10.				

Figure 3.3 Blank structured observation sheet

Teacher Questioning to Assess Student Thinking

I have already suggested that teacher questions act as controlling moves in conversations, steering them in one direction or another. However, if used carefully they can be an important tool for teachers in gaining insight into children's thinking processes. They should be used with caution because:

- only one child generally answers at a time. This can be avoided by:

  - giving children time to respond, discussing their thinking in pairs or in small groups

  - giving choice between answers and asking children to vote

  - all children write an answer, and the teacher reads a selected few;

- some children can be passive whilst others answer all the questions. Thus, targeted questions, accounting for attainment, should be asked of specific children;

- overlong question and answer sessions can lead to unrest and disruption.

Good Practice Point

Extending Children's Answers

Questions often produce short, limited answers. To extend these:

- ask 'open' rather than 'closed' questions;

- ask children to elaborate;

- repeat or 'echo' their answer;

- add a contribution from your own experience;

- clarify, suggest, reflect, add more information and speculate.

Children's thinking activities for specific aspects of their purposeful thinking can be explored using the prompts in Figure 3.4.

Further, the level of children's thinking in their responses to broader conceptual questions, whether written or oral, can be analysed using the Structure of Observed Learning Outcomes (SOLO) taxonomy[1] (indeed, the SOLO criteria can also be matched to statements in observation records to describe the quality of discourse in relation to levels of thinking). An adapted version of this taxonomy is summarized in Figure 3.5, and below I provide a case study of how it might be used.

Thinking purpose	Related activities	Examples of questions
Descriptive: searching for meaning	Sequencing, ordering, ranking Sorting, classifying, grouping Analysing, parts-whole, compare-contrast, similarities and differences	What is the best way to order them? What do we need to know about them to order them? How are these items similar or different?
Critical judgement: going beyond the information given	Making predictions, hypothesizing Drawing conclusions, reasons for conclusions Distinguishing fact from opinion Determining bias, reliability of evidence Relating cause and effect, designing a fair test	What might happen? What evidence indicates this? What conclusions can you reach here? How do you know you can believe this? Why should I believe you? What might have caused this to happen? Have you tested this fairly? Are there any other explanations? How might we test them?
Creative: suspending judgement	Generating ideas and possibilities Building and combining ideas Formulating own points of view Taking multiple perspectives and seeing others' points of view	What alternative ways can we approach this problem? What things are stopping us in each case? How have other people tackled this? Why have they tried things differently?
Problem-solving and evaluative	Identifying problems Thinking up different solutions Testing out solutions Planning	What do we need to do here? What is stopping us from doing it? What options do we have? What other things do we need to consider?
Decision-making	Making decisions Generating options Weighing up pros and cons Reviewing consequences	What are the priorities here? What are the consequences of each option? Which option balances pros and cons? Which option provides the best solution?

Figure 3.4 Questions relating to specific thinking activities

Stage	Descriptor	Evaluative criteria – features of responses
1	Pre-structural	Confused or irrelevant responses; Responses do not relate to the question (does not remember question, says 'I don't know', restates the question, makes a guess as to what response is required); wish to finish quickly without even considering the problem.
2	Unistructural	Makes use of one relevant point or feature; generalizes in terms of one aspect; finishes quickly, conclusions inconsistent, and jumps to conclusions on one aspect.
3	Multi-structural	Involves two or more relevant points or features but does not link them which may result in inconsistency especially when drawing conclusions; generalizes in terms of a few limited aspects.
4	Relational	Involves and relates two or more relevant points or features and gives an overall concept or principle; generalizes well within a given context. No inconsistency within context, but may be when going into other contexts.

Figure 3.5 The SOLO taxonomy

CASE STUDY

Using SOLO

As an example of how this taxonomy might be applied, I consider children's responses to the question, 'Were children's lives good in England in Victorian times?'

At the lowest (pre-structural) level children provided irrelevant answers such as, 'Of course not. They didn't have televisions or anything like that. It must have been so boring.'

In a unistructural response the child's point of view is supported by only one piece of evidence. So the child might say or write, 'Children's lives were horrible. They had to work from 6 years of age and had terrible conditions. They worked for long periods of time and their jobs were very dangerous. Some children were killed. Nowadays we don't have to do that. We are lucky, we can go to school.'

Multi-structural responses include two or more pieces of unrelated evidence to support the child's point of view. Thus the child might say, 'I don't think that children's lives were good because they were beaten and treated badly. In Victorian times people were very strict. In school you had the cane and had to wear a dunce's cap if you were naughty. Also children had to work, and the jobs were hard, dirty and sometimes dangerous.'

Finally, at the relational response level points are presented from both sides of an argument. Thus the child might write, 'In Victorian times children were treated like adults. Poor children had to go to work and rich children spent very little time with their parents. They even dressed like grown ups. They were sent away to school. Poor children sometimes had dangerous jobs, and many were killed, but some factory owners were kind and fed the children. Some took in orphans from the streets of the cities and gave them jobs in their factories and gave them a bed in a house nearby. I don't think it would have been as much fun being a child then.'

There is a fifth level within the SOLO taxonomy, the extended abstract. In this the learner considers many features and relates these to each other and to abstract principles. However, as this applies almost entirely to older learners, I have not included an example of it here.

Metacognition

If we are serious about developing learners who are internally driven to want to learn, and whose intention in learning is to make meaning and develop their understanding, then we must encourage them to exert control over their own learning. The process of reflecting on and controlling our own learning is called metacognition, and involves the following processes.

Preparing for Learning

To prepare themselves for learning, children can consider the nature of the learning task, the situation in which the task and learning is taking place and the ways in which success in the task will be appraised and learning assessed. Thus they might:

- think of possible learning goals, the ways in which they will go about the task, the resources they will need, the time they have and their existing prior knowledge;

- decide on a plan of action based on the above information.

Monitoring, Testing and Diagnosing

During the learning process, children will appraise whether things are going according to plan. This will involve:

- monitoring whether the learning process is actually taking them in the right direction (identifying areas they do not understand, which are not clear, which contradict other information they have, which do not fit with their experience, and so on);

- testing or checking whether they understand something thoroughly, for example, talking themselves through it, teaching it to someone else or trying to apply it to novel situations;

- diagnosing the gaps in their knowledge and mastery by, for example, considering why they are finding something difficult.

Adjusting

This involves the learner returning to their initial learning plan and making changes in the light of monitoring, testing or checking and diagnosing. This might lead the learner to:

- ask for help;

- pay extra attention or return to aspects of their learning;

- widen their knowledge base;

- changing their learning goals;

- spend more time on some areas of learning whilst skipping others.

Evaluating and Reflecting

Finally, we might ask whether the planned learning goals were achieved, whether other unplanned learning goals were achieved, by what process this happened and whether it could have been improved.

Linking Metacognitive Approaches to Assessment

Assessment is a powerful arena for the promotion and use of metacognitive processes. In the following sections I describe some common assessment practices, illustrating how they can be subtly adapted to provide opportunities for children's metacognitive processes.

Learning Intentions

We cannot plan learning activities without considering the kind of things we would like children to learn from them. These intended outcomes are referred to here as learning intentions. In recent years much has been made of the role of learning intentions in facilitating teachers' formative assessment and children's self-assessments. But it is important that we also encourage children to formulate their own intentions for their learning, and this is often missed in suggestions for good practice.

Good Practice Point

Whose Learning Intentions?

For many teachers, their formative assessments address how well children have met the particular intended outcomes planned for activities and lessons. However, learning is a complex process, and children may learn in ways which teachers can neither foresee nor determine. Nevertheless, sharing teacher intentions with children at the start of lessons can have a number of benefits. It helps children to understand the rationale for their work and allows them to evaluate the extent to which learning tasks address the learning which they are designed to address. It therefore increases child ownership of learning tasks and, as a result, children tend to be more engaged in tasks, persevering for longer and wasting less time. As a consequence the quality of student work improves.

However it is also important that we engage children in a dialogue about the intentions they have for their own learning. This might be in the form of reflecting on targets which they have set for themselves or negotiated with their teachers or, as a result of a consideration of how they feel about an area of learning already, identifying what areas they now need to address.

Further, by engaging in a dialogue with children around learning intentions and the actual learning resulting from engagement in particular tasks, both peer and self-assessment skills can be developed. The use and discussion of teacher marking which focuses on evidence for the achievement of particular learning intentions can support this process.

Teacher Feedback and Marking

Marking is important because it is a direct form of written feedback relating to the product of children's work, resulting from the planned lessons.

Feedback is sometimes one way, with the teacher providing an expert judgement which is accessible to the learner, who is given time to read, reply to and act upon comments. However, it is more effective when the work is marked in partnership with the child, and this should be the case whenever possible. This partnership supports the learner in developing their skills of self-reflection through a collaborative dialogue. It involves processes such as:

- making connections between what has been learnt in different contexts;

- reflecting on one's own learning and learning strategies;

- exploring how the learning contexts have played a part in making the learning effective;

- setting further learning goals;

- engaging with others in learning.

Good Practice Point

Ways of Making Effective Use of Teacher Feedback and Marking

1. Feedback and marking are often more useful if:

   (a) they are based on both the teacher's and the child's clear learning intentions (see previous section) before considering achievement beyond the learning intentions;

   (b) children are asked to produce self-evaluations first (or to peer mark in pairs – see later). This can be encouraged using questions such as:

       (i) What did you find easy?

       (ii) Where did you get stuck and what helped you?

       (iii) What do you need more help with?

       (iv) What are you most pleased with?

       (v) Have you learnt anything new?

       (vi) How would you change this activity with another group?

       (vii) Do you have any questions?

2. Extensive marking should only be given to longer or more complex pieces of work, not to every piece of work. When possible, feedback should be given orally. In this:

   (a) consideration can also be given to the child's self-evaluation;

   (b) the future learning goals in the form of targets and support to meet them are negotiated.

3. Feedback should not be in the form of grades:

   (a) Areas of success and for improvement can be highlighted.

   (b) Suggested strategies for improvement are provided.

   (c) Achievable short-term targets or 'next steps' to be met are suggested.

Good Practice Point

Some Specific Considerations in Relation to Children's Writing

1. When marking extended writing, identify two good parts of the work and one for development. Ask the child to do the same (perhaps on a photocopy). Discussion and comments can then relate specifically to these particular sections.

2. Teacher comments on written work will focus on developing a critically reflective dialogue by raising questions and making suggestions.

3. Comments addressing secretarial (including presentational) features of student work should be limited to a few features and be based on identified learning intentions.

Teacher–Student Conferences

Conferences are focused conversations between teachers and children about particular pieces of children's work. They can focus on providing a negotiated assessment of the work, and they also enable children to learn from their own reflections and allow teachers to model and support this. Regular short one-to-one conferences with teachers have been found to be more helpful than fewer longer ones.

Good Practice Point

Managing Teacher–Student Conferences

Remembering the effects of teacher control on their conversations with children and therefore on children's thinking, it is important in conferences that teachers let the children lead the way. An open question might begin the process, such as: 'can you tell me something about this work?' or 'can you tell me the story of this work?' Whilst listening to children, the teacher might:

- check they have understood the sense of what the child is saying by repeating the child's phrases and asking if that is what they meant, by asking what they meant – can they say it in a different way – and by asking for clarification on uncertainties;

- draw attention to something they feel is relevant;

- respond to and so encourage the child to say more, to go on with the train of thought;

- extend the sense of what the child has said by prompting the child to recognize patterns, make links, and recognize the consequences and implications of their assertions;

- notice a possible error, inconsistency or problem which the child has overlooked and prompt the child to look again;

- offer reassurance, praise, or other encouragement, either to celebrate what has been achieved or to motivate the child to persevere.

Conferences are models of critically reflective thinking. Of course, the more often children engage in such conversations, the more skilled they will become and the less reliant they will be on the teacher's support. To reinforce this it is worthwhile to, initially, following a conference, ask the child to write a report on the critical reflections which arose in the conference, but later, as the child becomes more experienced, ask the child to produce such a report before the conference to act as a starting point for this.

These conversations are learning processes because, as the child is reflecting upon their work, they are, amongst other things, clarifying ideas, identifying links, making new understandings and recognizing and trying to resolve contradictions. Thus, children are changing their perspective on their work in the course of the conference. The teacher's supportive interactions further help this process by prompting the child's own reflections to address these areas and by modelling the process when necessary. This is a process of supporting the development of the child's own reflective internal dialogue to further their learning.

Use the conference summary sheet in Task 3.3 to record the outcomes of a conference you have conducted. At the end of the conference, a few areas can be highlighted by both teacher

Task 3.3 Teacher–student conferencing

Use the blank conference summary sheet below to conduct a conference as described in the main text.

Name:	Class:	Date:
Area	**Student comments**	**Teacher comments**
What have I done well in my work? In which areas of my learning could I improve? Which areas of my learning could I explain to another person? Which areas of my learning couldn't I explain? Which areas can I make use of elsewhere? Which areas of my learning do I still need to practise using in class? What do I need to learn next?		

Negotiated targets:

■

■

■

Signed (teacher):	Signed (student):

Write your own reflections on the process of conferencing, including:

■ How willing were the children to reflect?

■ How difficult was it for you to let the children lead the way?

■ How reflective and how descriptive were the comments the children eventually made?

■ Which strategies were most effective in encouraging children's engagement and reflection?

Using Thinking Skills in the Primary Classroom © Kelly, 2005

and child as being of particular significance. Short-term achievable targets can be negotiated for these areas, and the teacher and child can discuss the means available (resources, opportunities, people) to support the child in working towards meeting these targets.

Peer Assessment

As with conferences, peer assessment is an educative process: an opportunity for thoughtfulness, reflection and profound thinking. Concerns about honesty and trustworthiness in peer assessment have to be weighed against sensitivity about self-esteem and confidence levels of the people receiving the feedback.

Good Practice Point

Ways of Introducing and Making Use of Peer Assessment

1. Children need training in peer assessment. This is best done in a small group, with the teacher modelling the role of the peer assessor with a specific example of student work. To do this the teacher follows the process outlined in 2 below, making clear their thoughts and, in particular, the thinking processes leading to decisions and judgements. One at a time, the children can then take turns to be the teacher with the teacher supporting them.

2. Ground rules need to be established in groups. Essential prerequisites include: all in the group must listen, there should be no interruptions, and both confidentiality and sensitivity should be maintained. Other important rules include:

   (a) group members should take turns to point out what they like first (and highlight these) against the learning intentions, whilst the child who produced the work listens;

   (b) taking turns in the group, children might then say, 'I agree with another member's assessment because … ' or 'I disagree because … ', as well as adding new viewpoints including some points for development;

   (c) in all, three positive features should be identified for every one requiring improvement;

   (d) after all members have contributed the child who produced the work can respond.

3. Paired or partnership oral marking involves children choosing a suitable partner with whom to discuss their work and comment on each others' work. Partners should trust each other, and should not include pairs who are both low-attaining children.

4. In the paired model, the assessor can be called a response partner. They are someone who:

   (a) talks about the child's work in relation to the specific success criteria;

   (b) makes the child feel good by pointing out what they have done well;

   (c) suggests to the child how they could improve their work.

Student Learning Diaries

Student learning diaries about their classroom learning experiences are important because they can be used to provide feedback from the child's perspective, and can help in identifying individual student problems. They can contribute significantly to increasing student motivation, enjoyment and understanding.

Essentially the diary, which should be completed regularly and whenever the child wants to, becomes a private conversation between the teacher and the child. It also acts as a basis for children's developing self-evaluative skills.

Children need support in learning how to use the diaries. These should record children's views and feelings about their experiences of learning. Training will include negotiation with the children to agree:

- who will have access to the diaries – normally only the teacher who will keep the contents of the diary confidential (see issue 3 below);

- whether the teacher will have access to the whole diary or only part of it;

- whether access should ever be shared with other children or not – if, for example, a shared anxiety is raised;

- how often diaries will be written in by children (normally daily or every two days) and read by teachers (normally weekly or fortnightly);

- how the teacher should respond to their comments – normally by writing in the diary, but sometimes also by writing somewhere else, talking with the child or in some other way;

- any other issues raised by the children.

Diaries normally develop through use and through the way in which they are dealt with and responded to by teachers. Where child comments are valued and acted upon, and where diaries are seen to be important to teachers, children value them and use them appropriately.

Good Practice Point

Issues for Consideration with Diaries

1. Diaries are a two-way process, with teachers raising issues and thoughts with children as much as children do so with teachers.
2. It is necessary to give diaries time to work, because a rapport and sense of trust needs to develop between child and teacher.
3. It is important to consider as a school how the teacher should respond to personal issues or areas of concern revealed in the diary. Children should know that teachers may have to seek advice or talk to others if they are overly concerned about anything revealed in the diary.
4. Diaries also provide an opportunity to explore areas of understanding with children. This can be initiated by a child raising areas of confusion or misunderstanding with the teacher, or by the teacher informally asking the child about their thoughts in relation to a particular area.

Student Portfolios

A portfolio is a product, a document which records a range of assessment information from a wide variety of contexts (such as that indicated in this document). Portfolios are important because they:

- provide a summative record of achievement which includes consideration of the process of learning as well as the product, the progression of learning over time and the influence of context on learning;

- provide personal knowledge and promote positive attitudes (greater insight into themselves as learners; a feeling of greater control over learning; increased motivation to inspire future learning);

- develop personal skills (improved communication skills, increased confidence in articulating personal ideas and achievements);

- and contribute towards the school's evaluation of teaching and curriculum organization.

A portfolio is a collection of work which:

- acts as a basis for and record of student self-evaluation and reflection;

- provides an opportunity to portray the processes by which the work in the portfolio is achieved;

- includes assessment of performance in real situations.

Profiling is the process by which the portfolio is produced: individual reflection, self-assessment, review discussions to evaluate attainment, acknowledge success and failure, and discuss performance in relation to learning outcomes. This can result in target–setting and action planning.

Good Practice Point

Ways of Developing and Using Student Portfolios

1. During the course of the year, collect together significant work from each subject, each in a separate folder, arranged temporally to show development and progression.
2. Work could include formative assessments such as teacher and student marking, student self-evaluations, conference records, peer assessment discussion summaries and redrafts.
3. At particular times during the year, children should consider the work in their portfolios, recognizing and evaluating their own progress and development, and setting longer-term targets for improvement in each subject area.
4. The portfolio can also include records of other, non-academic, achievements such as sports certificates.

Reflection Point

A Note on Student Self-assessment

Self-assessments based on simple questionnaires, asking, for example, 'what part of the work did you find easiest or hardest', tend to be descriptive rather than reflective and evaluative. It is only through supported opportunities for reflection such as those described in this chapter that children can learn to develop a reflective approach.

> Similarly, without support, pupils tend to judge their own attainment and progress through comparison with their classmates. To some extent sharing 'child-speak' criteria enables the emphasis to move towards achievement in relation to those criteria rather than comparison with peers. However providing children with opportunities to evaluate their own work on the basis of particular criteria and to compare their own work with that of others and with examples of quality work enables them to better understand the criteria to which they are working.

Recording and Reporting

Finally, it should be added that the recording and reporting of children's achievements should be based on the same principles as those for the processes of assessment. Thus recording and reporting should:

- consider all aspects of learning and individual development, not simply those which are testable. This includes knowledge, skills and understandings, but also areas such as attitudes and beliefs, communicative and collaborative skills, social skills, learning processes and thinking;

- consider learners differential attainment in different contexts, and should show attainment within a complex picture of progressive development rather than as a simple snapshot;

- be based on as wide a variety of approaches as possible, but should bear in mind the limitations of each approach. As often as possible these should involve learners as reflective participants in the process;

- be a participative process, respectful of a learning partnership between pupils, parents and teachers, and focus on the development of reflective dialogues.

So, as an example in relation to the last bullet point, in a pupil–parent–teacher conference the child might set the agenda and chair the meeting, beginning by offering their own reflections on key areas of their learning – based on portfolio evidence – and then asking for parent and teacher comments and reflections before negotiating new learning targets or goals.

Thinking Assessment

In this chapter we have considered the key role that assessment has in promoting children's use of their thinking skills in the classroom. As Walter Doyle said in 1983, children exchange 'performance for grades',[2] meaning that they try to do what they think the teacher wants them to do, and what the teacher assesses is a key indicator of this. Thus, and this cannot be overstated, if we want to promote thoughtful approaches then we must assess thoughtful approaches, and we must do it in a thoughtful way.

Key Points

1. Assessment is a reflective log of events and our response to them, a record of our changing selves.

2. For assessment to enable us to shape rounded and thoughtful individuals whose learning reaches out from the classroom to engage with the world:

   (a) teachers should assess what they value, and not simply concentrate on what is easiest to assess, including attitudes, beliefs, understandings and skills;

   (b) teachers should assess the same knowledge in a variety of contexts, both schooling and other, and over a period of time, recognizing that context and time are issues;

   (c) teachers should ensure that they use a variety of observational, oral, discursive and written approaches, including testing, to make both formative and summative assessments of learning;

   (d) children, parents and teachers should consider all these assessment approaches and issues when making overall judgements.

3. For assessment to encourage thoughtful approaches and deep engagement we must:

   (a) consider the process of learning and not just the product

   (b) engage in approaches which encourage children to explain and try to understand their reasoning

   (c) discuss problems so that children reveal their ways of thinking.

4. For assessment to promote a love of learning for its own sake, and encourage learners to enter their learning with an intention to understand, and for assessment to be part of that learning process, developing metacognitive and reflective approaches:

   (a) children should be regarded as partners in the learning process and be involved in extended assessment dialogues with teachers, friends and parents;

   (b) teacher feedback should be dialogic and promote a learning partnership with the child.

5. Assessment is a powerful arena for the promotion and use of metacognitive processes. Approaches which promote metacognition include:

   (a) sharing teacher and pupil learning intentions;

   (b) discursive feedback and marking;

   (c) teacher–student conferences;

   (d) peer assessment;

   (e) student learning diaries;

   (f) student portfolios.

6. Principles for recording and reporting children's achievements should be the same as those for the processes of assessment.

CHAPTER 4

Promoting Disciplined Thinking Skills Through Authentic Activity

Life on the Production Line

Chapter 1 describes an apt metaphor for busy, pacey and accountable classrooms: the industrial production line. In this, the teacher (or supervisor) controls the transmission of ready-made packages of knowledge by providing appropriate tasks, and then monitors and assesses their acquisition. The pupils (or labour force) work to complete these tasks. Classrooms like this are 'work' centred rather than 'learning' centred, and children see the usefulness of their learning in these same narrow terms: learning is important so that you know what to do in your work, so you get better at your work and so you pass examinations. In this chapter I consider ways in which we can create purposeful contexts for activity and enquiry in our classrooms.

There are many productive metaphors that we can adopt for our classrooms: the writer's workshop, the artist's studio, the scientist's laboratory and so on. These allow children to act as craft apprentices rather than unskilled labourers. This chapter explores some of these metaphors. In each case it is suggested that the children engage in the authentic activities of the community to which the metaphor pertains. I will begin by considering how children can engage in the authentic activities of academic disciplines.

Reflection Point

Promoting Disciplined Thinking

There is a distinction between 'academic disciplines' and 'school subjects', which I believe is helpful in that it suggests changes in practice that might promote thoughtful engagement with key ideas in the area of study rather than just participation in lessons – thus bringing about deeper learning.

The term 'academic discipline' carries much baggage and cannot be characterized in a simplistic way. I use 'discipline' here to represent the distinctive approaches or ways of thinking of academic communities exploring their knowledge of particular aspects of the world. These approaches have been described in terms of the processes of, for example, historical, scientific, technological or textual analysis, guided by the established theories and ideas of the field of enquiry. Further, such communities through their discipline may affirm, verify or contend existing knowledge or create knowledge through their working practices, and communicate (through

various methods of discourse – debate, publication and so on) these activities to a wider audience for validation, perhaps contributing towards a consensus of opinion. Although this all sounds complex, in essence it can be stated simply: academic disciplines are what academics know and do, be they scientists, historians, or the like.

Academic disciplines differ from school subjects in that the purpose of activity within a disciplined community is the creation, sharing, validation and application of ideas. The focus is the knowledge and its integrity, not the integrity of the person who holds it. School subjects do not, on the whole, affirm, verify or contend existing knowledge or create knowledge, they transmit it in ready-made packages. It is the working practices of school that are adopted in this, with the acquisition of predetermined knowledge being the goal. The teacher controls the transmission of knowledge and assesses its acquisition, sometimes through teacher assessment, and sometimes by means of standardized testing.

At this point an example might help. The story of the good samaritan is one frequently taught to show how Jesus illustrated the Christian view that people should 'love thy neighbour as thyself'. In the school subject Religious Education (RE), we might explore this parable, learn what a parable is, look at the meanings within the story, discuss the significance of each character within the story and relate it to contemporary events (amongst many other things, which I am sure creative teachers would present in an inviting and captivating way). The main emphasis is on certain relevant 'received wisdom' about these parables being communicated to the children in a way which they can relate to, understand, and apply to new contexts. In contrast, an approach to this through the academic disciplines of hermeneutics or exegesis might seek to explore the parable in its original context (using information from other sources) and, in so doing, question existing interpretations of the story, try and raise new interpretations, consider novel applications and communicate new ideas to a critical audience for their commentary.

This example suggests that the belief systems of activity within each academic disciplines and school subjects also differ. In Chapter 1 I suggested that being a pupil involves learning to perform (that is, work) well on school tasks within the context of schooling, and I described a number of strategies helpful to pupils, including using language which conforms to the required classroom conventions and understanding the assessment systems within the classroom so as to put one's energies into meeting these rather than spending too much time on things which are not assessed and therefore not rewarded. In short, being a pupil involves learning the working practices of school.

On the other hand, being, for example, a historian involves seeing the world through a historian's eyes, and describing it thus: in challenging existing ways of doing this and providing new ways; in providing a greater understanding of humanity and fresh insights into what it is to be human. Thus, in Chapter 1 I provided the example of an historian who, considering Germany during the Second World War might ask, 'What does the Holocaust tell us about the human experience or condition?' and 'How can the Holocaust help us to understand the human experience or condition better?'

School Knowledge, Academic Disciplines and the Question of Usefulness

The usefulness of school knowledge is mostly viewed by schoolchildren in the narrow terms of their schooling: learning is important so that you know what to do in your work, so you get better at your work and so you pass examinations. Children can think perfectly well in school as well as out of school, but in school much of their thinking is blinkered by the working practices of school already described.

CASE STUDY

An Example of a Local History Project with the Community

What might this look like in practice? It requires learners to engage in the authentic activities of the relevant academic discipline, adopting the same goals as people working within the discipline. Thus the first and foremost goal of this authentic activity is not individual learning (although this is a useful side product). For example, in geography an authentic activity might involve conducting a census or survey to research changes in the local population. This information might be used to forecast school population growth and changes in the demand for other local amenities. Such an enquiry might then inform an aspect of future planning. During this work experts might be brought in to model and support children in their activity.

It is evident from the above example that activities chosen as authentic for a discipline should:

■ involve children in using the key ideas and tools of the subject in an enquiry for which the answer is not already known;

■ involve enquiry which is purposeful, and aim to meet such purposes;

■ be intelligible to those involved;

■ involve a partnership with others who have an interest or expertise in the object or process of enquiry.

One example of an authentic historical activity is a local community history project in which pupils worked with parents, grandparents, members of the local community and local historians, to create a community history.

Adults and children worked alongside each other in this project which was carried out in an inner city primary school with pupils from year 6. Initially a range of databases (including the archives of the local newspaper at their offices) were searched to identify key themes. These themes arose from the response of each group to the data that they were looking at. Thus, one group became interested in the effect of the 1832 cholera epidemic on the city in which they lived when they read an article about this in a local newspaper.

Each group, made up of a supportive adult and six pupils, then targeted particular time periods and/or themes, gathering and considering any available evidence from primary and secondary sources whilst noting questions of interest to follow up. Thus it was identified that the cholera epidemic was exacerbated by the squalid conditions in which many lived and that population movements might have been a significant factor in the spread of the disease. The group set about mapping this in their own community. A search of hospital records, local church records and graveyards produced some interesting possibilities with surnames suggesting that many Irish people contracted the disease. When a picture was beginning to emerge, knowledge gaps were identified and decisions made as to how these might best be filled. In some cases this required experts or witnesses (such as local historians and epidemiologists) to be interviewed, and further evidence to be sought out.

Finally, ideas were brought together and eventually published in a community history, each group contributing one chapter on their chosen theme – where previously there had been no written history. In the case of the group above, this was a description of the effect of the cholera epidemic on the community.

In all, work on the project amounted to one afternoon per week for much of the autumn term and, following its completion, the resulting volume was published and sold through the local library.

Academic discipline knowledge, however, reaches out to explore the world, and so is useful in far wider terms. Indeed, I would contend that it is the disciplined thinking within an academic tradition which we should be promoting in education, rather than just the restrained thinking of school: if we want to encourage children to think beyond school and therefore use their learning beyond school then they have to adopt the working practices for which the use applies; if we want children to think as historians they have to act like historians by adopting the working practices of historians. The same is, of course, true for scientists or practitioners in any other area of enquiry.

However this does not mean simply that we should use, for example, historical enquiry in our classrooms, because such enquiry is still set in the working practices of school: predetermined knowledge, restricted explorations, school beliefs about correctness and purpose, a tendency of children to search for and follow cues, and a lack of risk-taking. It means that we should allow our children to actually be historians.

Task 4.1 contains a list of disciplines which look at, enquire about and represent the world. Consider each one and how children could engage in the activities of people such as poets, composers or artists, with support at school. If you find this difficult, there are three case studies in this chapter which might provide some ideas.

Making Use of Scientific Enquiry

I now use the example of science and children working as scientists to illustrate how disciplined thinking and enquiry can be promoted in a variety of contexts. The concepts and methods of science can be applied to many contexts, and it is likely that there are some important benefits to setting learning in various different purposeful contexts: by making learning meaningful to learners, teachers may be more likely to promote positive cognitive change involving the movement from unhelpful beliefs and ideas about science to those which are more generally applicable and useful. With this in mind I describe two attempts at modelling how scientific enquiry might be used away from the classroom, each developing aspects of children's understanding of science in a different context. The first involves a vocational setting – a garden centre – and the second requires the use of science in another discipline – archaeology.

CASE STUDY

The Garden Centre

Following a visit to a local garden centre, a class of year 1 and 2 children decided to set up a garden centre in school, so that they could grow a variety of plants to sell in time for the summer fair.

Before this the children had been growing sunflowers from seed in class, exploring the conditions in which these would grow best. Following their explorations, hypotheses had been made as to which factors were most important in influencing plant growth. Factors suggested by the children included frequency and amount of watering for each plant, the soil type in each plant pot and the position of the plant in the classroom. Next, separate groups had chosen to investigate the effects of one of these factors on plant growth. Thus one group decided to water one sunflower with 100 mls of water daily, another every two days, and a third only

Task 4.1 Authentic activities

Look at the list of disciplines which look at, enquire about and represent the world. For each one, identify an authentic activity which children could engage in with support at school.

Disciplined community	Authentic activity
Composers and/or musicians	
Geographers	
Historians	
Mathematicians	
Painters and/or sculptors	
Playwrights and actors	
Poets	
Scientists	

when the compost in its pot was completely dry, in each case keeping all other conditions the same. This group of children had then engaged in an interesting debate about which effects should be measured: some wanted simply to look at the rate of growth for each plant – by measuring height or counting new leaves each day – whilst others wanted to identify the most healthy plant in terms of factors such as the girth of its stem and the colour of its leaves. Eventually height in millimetres was chosen as the main indicator, although a diary of descriptive statements about how healthy each plant looked was also kept.

The development of a class garden centre provided an ideal context for developing and applying some of the scientific ideas already encountered through the sunflower work. After working out how long they had until the fair, the proprietor of the local garden centre, Elaine, was approached for advice. She suggested that the children could germinate pansies, petunias and geraniums from seed, selling the seedlings in pots at the fair. These would take about a month to grow to the required size. The children could also provide the buyers with instructions for caring for these plants.

Although the findings of the children's previous investigations were interesting in relation to sunflowers (broadly speaking, water every two days, plant in potting compost and grow in a 'sunny' area of the class-room), the children appreciated that the most favourable conditions for growth would vary from plant to plant. Thus, they checked that the conditions that helped sunflowers grow were also best for the other plants by comparing their findings with the advice given in several gardening manuals. This led them to decide on the best growing conditions, given the limitations of the school environment, for each plant type.

The children then worked to grow sufficient seedlings for the fair. Germinating large amounts of seeds was not an easy process, and the children needed frequent support and expert advice from Elaine. Their activity was purposeful in making use of their growing understanding of plants to care for the seedlings. Their records served to inform others about caring for the seedlings, and the whole class shared in the success of growing enough healthy seedlings for the school summer fair.

CASE STUDY

Archaeology in the Classroom

The second example of a context for using scientific enquiry bridges history and science: a class of year 3 and 4 children became archaeologists, working closely with Rob, an archaeologist, for a day.

During the morning Rob explained the working practices of archaeologists to the children. He described the type, range and variety of evidence available to archaeologists, and discussed with the children the inferences that could be made from this evidence. Thus, in terms of mapping the countryside long ago, using evidence available today, the children were introduced to the following:

- Pollen: under the right circumstances this can survive for thousands of years. It can be dated and used to identify the species of plant occupying a particular locality at a particular time.

- Snail shells: these can be dated and used to identify the type of snail living in a particular place at a particular time. This information can, in turn, be used to infer the type of habitat (for example, grassland, woodland) of the place at that time.

■ Animal bones: these can be used to identify the animals present at a time.

■ Wheat seeds: these provide evidence of farming.

■ Building artefacts: these provide evidence of settlement.

■ Aeriel views and land shape: this can provide evidence of human changes made to the land.

Similarly, in terms of human remains, Rob explained how clues such as the head size, bone shape and the number of teeth could be used to infer the person's gender, build, age, health and wealth. The nature of burial also provides clues: a sixth–eighth century body buried in an East–West position is likely to be Christian (and consequently Saxon), whereas one buried at the same time North–South is more likely to be pagan (and Viking). A body buried face down is likely to have been executed.

In the afternoon the children became archaeologists for themselves. In small teams they were presented with a variety of items that had been found in a 'dig', and had to sort and classify these, paying particular attention to their similarities and differences. Then they used these observations to draw inferences and conclusions about the artefacts' identity and use. For example, various pieces of pottery were included, and the children had to group these before deciding whether it was used for cooking, storage or eating from. They deduced this by considering the thickness, size, glaze, colour and texture of the piece. Similar consideration was given to other items including building materials such as tile, brick, mosaic and nails.

During the day there were plenty of opportunities for the expert, Rob, to instruct and then support the activity of the children, who were acting as apprentice archaeologists. The children's activity was purposeful – they were using evidence to make inferences about the past. Their activity was evaluated on group success, achieved through sharing information and supporting each other, and not on individual success. Finally, their records, using charts, tables and drawings, enabled them to share information and discuss ideas: it was not simply to show that they had been busy working.

In all three of the case studies above, the activities chosen for making use of scientific or historical processes and ideas should also:

■ involve children using the key ideas of science and the tools of scientists in an enquiry for which the answer is not readily available from other sources;

■ involve an enquiry with a clear purpose;

■ involve a partnership with others who have an interest or expertise in the object or process of enquiry.

Return to Task 4.1, and consider each of the areas of authentic activity again. Can you think of a variety of contexts for each one? For example, the authentic activities of poets could be adopted in a poetry week resulting in the production of a school anthology of poems for sale to parents. Alternatively, the children could write poems for a celebratory event such as a school anniversary. However, children might also be allowed the opportunity to write poetry for themselves, describing their experiences, emotions and responses to their everyday lives.

Looking Through Many Eyes

In Chapter 1 I described a research study which I carried out looking at whether a primary pupil's learning about a particular theme or concept in history differs substantively if it occurs within the context of, say, a drama lesson than if it occurs within a literacy hour, and concluded that, whilst subjects benefit from being addressed as disciplines in their own right, much can also be gained by looking at conceptual areas through various subjects. So in a historical study of the Battle of the Somme in 1916, children could engage in not only a historical enquiry based approach, be it text or computer based or involving the examination of original artefacts, but also in looking at events through the eyes of poets and novelists, or through the eyes of geographers or scientists. As such, the work of others might be explored, and the children might engage in original work themselves not only in writing and poetry, but also through the media of music, dance, drama and painting. This rich experience is more than simply engaging children with history, or encouraging them to use their thinking skills in school: it helps bring people towards an understanding of our shared humanity, of the human condition.

The Key Features of Authentic Activity and Enquiry in the Classroom

In order to promote ways of thinking that are useful beyond school we must teach children in ways which take their learning beyond the narrow terms of school and help them to reach out and explore the world. One way of doing this is to adopt the working practices of academic disciplines. So, in the previous examples of history and science, this might be by helping children to do some or all of the following:

- engage in the authentic activities of historians or scientists;

- affirm, verify or contend, and apply existing historical or scientific knowledge or create and validate new knowledge;

- communicate (through various methods of discourse – debate, publication, and so on) their activities to a wider audience for validation;

- contribute towards a consensus of opinion.

Staying with the examples of history and science, through these processes of authentic enquiry, learners are encouraged to develop beliefs in which they at least begin to:

- view history or science as ways of seeing the world, of looking through historical or scientific eyes, with, for instance, historical activity as requiring us to actually be historians;

- understand the 'big ideas' of a subject. This includes the biggest ideas of all – the essence of what a subject is about. Thus, subjects such as history, geography and RE are called the humanities because they are about understanding humanity, that is, the human experience and condition, be it temporally, spatially, culturally or spiritually; and science is about how people explain, understand and attempt to control their universe;

- realize that phenomena and events have many interpretations, taken from many perspectives, each of which might contribute to peoples' understandings and none of which, taken in isolation, are singularly true;

- realize that knowledge is constructed by people, and is necessarily fallible and transient in nature, and that the way in which knowledge is created is as important to our understanding of phenomena as the knowledge itself.

Lesson Ideas (with a suggested Thinking Skills Emphasis): Examples of Authentic Activities

For mathematics: conducting a traffic survey in order to provide evidence for a letter to the council for some form of traffic control outside school; costing and planning a residential visit; running a school stationary shop – ordering, pricing and selling goods in order to make a small profit. (*Possible Thinking Skills Emphasis: searching for meaning; making critical judgements; decision-making*)

In science children might: set up a weather station or get involved in monitoring environmental changes in an environmental awareness campaign; set up a local research group exploring migration or the insect population. (*Possible Thinking Skills Emphasis: making critical judgements; problem-solving; decision-making*) .

In geography, children might survey and research school population growth using various indicators such as local birth rates for forecasting, and identifying the implications of their findings. (*Possible Thinking Skills Emphasis: searching for meaning; making critical judgements; decision-making*)

Finally, in music the children might make a CD for sale following their composition of various items. (*Possible Thinking Skills Emphasis: being creative*)

Authentic Activity: Some Issues

This approach has obvious attractions, which I hope this chapter has made clear. However, it also sets us challenges, and as practitioners we must be constantly alert to these. Some of these questions schools must answer for themselves. These include: what is the relative place in school subjects of authentic activities and how can approaches complement each other? What is the right balance in learning environments between activities which address and monitor knowledge acquisition and activities which involve learners in knowledge creation and use?

In this chapter we have moved a long way away from the view that teaching thinking is filling an individual's 'learning bag' full of useful skills. Instead, we have considered how children can use their thinking skills to engage in the deep and disciplined thinking of particular knowledge-building communities. This is consistent with the view of learning, discussed in Chapter 1, as changing people by changing the way we understand and see the world. As such it is challenging but immensely worthwhile for us as educators.

Key Points

1. There are many more productive metaphors that we can adopt for our classrooms than the industrial production line: the writer's workshop, the artist's studio, the scientist's laboratory and so on.

2. It is useful to make the distinction between academic disciplines and school subjects.

3. Being a pupil involves learning to perform (that is, work) well on school tasks within the context of school.

4. Providing children with opportunities to engage in the authentic activities of academic disciplines allows them to reach out and explore their world.

5. Areas such as scientific enquiry can be used away from the classroom, each developing aspects of children's understanding of science in different contexts.

6. Primary pupil's learning about particular themes or concepts differs substantively if it occurs within the context of, say, a drama lesson than if it occurs within a literacy hour.

7. Through these processes of authentic activity and enquiry, learners are encouraged to develop beliefs in which they at least begin to:

   (a) view disciplines as ways of seeing or thinking about the world;

   (b) understand the 'big ideas' of a subject, including the biggest ideas of all — the essence of what a subject is about;

   (c) realize that phenomena and events have many interpretations, taken from many perspectives, each of which might contribute to peoples' understandings and none of which, taken in isolation, are singularly true;

   (d) realize that knowledge is constructed by people, and is necessarily fallible and transient in nature, and that the way in which knowledge is created is as important to our understanding of phenomena as the knowledge itself.

CHAPTER 5

Promoting Creativity

Perspectives on Creativity

For many involved in primary education, the promotion of children's creativity is of central importance. So, in recent years, a major criticism by educationalists of standards-driven educational reforms that focus on efficiency and rigour has been that they have limited the opportunities for promoting creativity and developing children's creative abilities.

Before we begin, reflect on your own views of what creativity is through Task 5.1 (next page). A number of activities are listed, and for each one decide what is creative in this, what must novices learn to gain expertise in this and how do they learn these? Then look across your answers and see if there are any patterns or emerging views on which you have made your decisions. How do these compare with the views described in the following Reflection Point?

Reflection Point

What Do We Mean by Creativity?

Just look through the pages of educational magazines or talk to groups of teachers and you will soon realize that creativity means many things to many people. To some extent the rather vague use of the term 'creativity' coupled with its rhetorical overuse in appealing for something better has devalued it: it has become something subscribed to by all but actively sought by only a few. Sometimes the word is used almost synonymously with the phrase 'child-centred': to promote children's creativity we must provide them with opportunities to make choices and allow them the freedom to work outside the limitations imposed by school structures, following their own drives and interests. At other times it is used as shorthand for the creative arts: painting, sculpture, drama, dance, music and so on. Here creativity might be promoted by allowing children the opportunity to engage more in such subject areas, perhaps working with experts such as artists in residence. But perhaps most significantly it is seen as the source of original thoughts, whether they are original just to the child who has never thought them before, or – in wider terms – whether they are original to the whole of humanity, a far rarer but nevertheless related event. In the main part such thoughts are seen by proponents of this view as goal directed, involving the solving of a problem, and therefore useful. Thus the National Advisory Committee on Creative and Cultural Education[1] promotes a view of creativity as 'imaginative activity fashioned so as to produce outcomes that are both original and of value.'

Task 5.1 What is creativity?

Consider the following activities. What would you consider creative action or production to look like in each of these, what would you see as being the essential attributes of the most creative participants, and how do you think those attributes have been developed?

Activity	What is creative in this?	What must novices learn to gain expertise in this?	How do they learn these?
Music – concert pianist			
Music – jazz and improvisation			
Painting			
Scientific research			
Sport – football			
Sport – gymnastics			
Writing – fantasy stories			
Writing – historical textbooks			
Writing – poetry			
Writing in a year 6 SATs test			

Using Thinking Skills in the Primary Classroom © Kelly, 2005

The first view, linking creativity to child-centredness, smacks of nostalgia – harking back to a rather romantic view of childhood where children's explorations and discoveries led them to insights on their world, untarnished by worldly experience or academic baggage. Theirs is what we might call a naive creativity. The second uses creativity simply as a label – separating learning and doing art or music for example from that in, say, mathematics or science – yet there are many who would say that they know musicians and artists whom they consider to be wholly technicist and uncreative, and scientists and mathematicians would add that their disciplines are full of opportunities for imaginative activity and originality. The third view has more potential as it allows creative endeavours across all areas of learning to be included and is appropriate to learners at all levels of expertise. It is this third perspective on creativity which I adopt in this chapter.

Reflect on the above and your response to Task 5.1. In your view, what is it that sets aside creative activity from other activities? What common attributes do creative performers from each separate area share? What is the role of expertise in each of these examples of creativity? Finally, which factors would appear to be significant in helping the development of creative performers? The remainder of this chapter addresses these points from the point of view of learning at school.

Thinking 'Outside the Box'

Having original thoughts involves thinking outside the box, whether the walls of the box represent the confines of particular approaches, perspectives, interpretations or even the classroom itself. But in education we tend to concentrate on how we can get children to think inside the box. Indeed, in Chapter 4 I described how we might encourage children to think as scientists, as historians, as poets and so on. So what is to be done?

Most generally, it is important that we promote and develop creative dispositions in children. So, to develop children who approach solving problems as original thinkers we should encourage them to be:

- enquiring: inquisitive, imaginative, enjoying exploration and investigation;

- active: goal orientated, willing to take risks, preferring complexity and accepting disorder;

- autonomous: independent, self-confident, internally controlled, persistent and flexible.

However, clues to effective approaches for supporting learners' creativity can also be gained when we consider what people need in order to be original in their thinking; what are the implications of preceding chapters in the context of those seeking novel solutions to problems? From these we can conclude that it is important for problem-solvers to:

- have a strong 'inner voice';

- accept uncertainty;

- work constantly on linking their thinking with understanding and solving problems in the real world;

- consider alternative perspectives on problems;

- be flexible in adopting more helpful ideas and perspectives and challenging less helpful ones;

- seek resolution of confusions or problems by sustained 'to-ing and fro-ing' from one perspective to another and back to the problem;

- accept multiple solutions.

In this chapter I consider how suggestions made elsewhere in this book can be built upon to encourage creativity-friendly dispositions and suggest creativity-friendly approaches.

Developing Creative Dispositions

Approaches adopted throughout this book have encouraged enquiring, active and autonomous learners, and as such are precursors for creative activity.

Enquiring and Active Learners

Enquiries such as those suggested in Chapters 2 and 4 enable learners to be inquisitive, imaginative, and enjoy exploration and investigation. They allow learners to engage in collaborative work in which they explore and investigate, considering alternative views and interpretations and form new views and interpretations. In these enquiries it is important that:

- children accept that, in the solution of problems or exploration of ideas there are genuine alternatives;

- the process of enquiry is not seen rigidly, but as a guiding template to be adapted to the particular circumstances of the enquiry;

- children are introduced to new ways of looking at problems and new ideas to help them in their work towards a solution;

- children are encouraged to look at their activity through the eyes of different perspectives: as a mathematician, a scientist, an engineer, an artist and so on;

- children are introduced to the notion of 'insight', where a solution to a problem can arise through a sudden realization that it can be viewed in a different way.

Two processes are important here. First, children should be encouraged to adopt a questioning stance. The questions they raise can mirror those in Figure 3.4, which could be used as prompts. They can be critical and evaluative, involving observing, comparing, recognizing similarities and differences, focusing, clarifying, analysing and investigating. On the other hand, they can generate new ideas through interpreting and explaining, seeking consequences and suggesting new problems to be explored. Such questioning stances are a central feature of the communities of, for example, historians, scientists and mathematicians whom we have discussed in the previous chapter, and will, of course, feature strongly when children engage in the activities of those communities.

Secondly, children should be encouraged to adopt an exploratory and investigative stance, playing with ideas (using a variety of approaches: making models, drawing pictures, drafting and redrafting texts, and so on) and engaging in dialogues where suggestions are made and considered speculatively. Nevertheless, despite having questioning and exploratory stances, discursive and authentic enquiries are orientated towards achieving particular goals. Also, as has been already suggested, children engaging in them need to show a willingness to take risks, understand that answers are seldom simple and more often complex, and accept disorder.

Thus discursive and authentic enquiries provide an ideal environment for the development of creative dispositions. But learners also need to be positively disposed towards autonomy.

Autonomous Learners

Autonomous learners are independent and self-directed. We might consider three levels of autonomy. The first is when learners have autonomy or control over the strategies which they use to carry out a task without the guidance of their teacher. Thus in mathematics a teacher might teach a variety of strategies for children to undertake three-digit multiplication. The children can then choose which one to use in tackling a problem. Similarly, children might choose the form of recording to use for a science exploration and so on. At the second level learners have control over the content of the curriculum, the things to be studied and learned, the objectives of learning. Thus, children might decide to explore something in its own right or set their own goals for their learning. They might choose an area or theme on history to research, an assignment to write, an experiment to do or a book to read. This is learning for pleasure, following tangents and satisfying curiosities. At the third level learners are able to judge things for themselves, after gathering evidence and taking various views into account. Thus the children might make informed decisions about changes to school routines such as playtimes, spending money on new items for class or elections to the school council. They might tackle controversial issues in school and debate these, looking at the perspectives of different parties.

This third level of autonomy goes beyond simply independence in accessing resources or completing the teachers' work, and has been called 'intellectual autonomy'.[2] Learners who have intellectual autonomy:

■ think for themselves;

■ link their thinking to their experiences;

■ open their minds to new ideas.

In Task 5.2 consider for each level of autonomy how you might encourage children through providing appropriate resources and teaching particular strategies. Which of these are your current practices and how might you extend them to take children towards the higher levels of autonomy?

Task 5.2 Encouraging autonomy

How might you encourage children to become more autonomous in their approaches to learning in terms of:

- the resources they might need?

- the strategies they might adopt?

Record your ideas below:

Degree of autonomy	Resource needs	Useful strategies
Autonomy of approach (Learners have control over the strategies which they use to carry out a task)		
Autonomy of focus (Learners have control over the content of the curriculum, the things to be studied and learned, the objectives of learning)		
Intellectual autonomy (Learners are able to judge things for themselves, after taking evidence and various views into account)		

Approaches which Allow and Encourage Creativity

Reflections on Creative People

In the introductory chapter of this book I discussed the work of JK Rowling, James Dyson and Vincent Van Gogh. Reflecting on their work I suggested it was important to recognize the place of time, persistence and expertise in their creativity. How does this match with your views on creativity following Task 5.1?

If we are to allow the children in our schools to also be creative, they too must have the time to do so, they must be encouraged to be persistent and resilient in their work and they must be engaged in developing their expertise in those areas which will contribute towards their creativity, be they knowledge, skills or understandings and ideas. But this raises a number of issues which schools must address, including how timetabling constraints affect the time children have available for this, and how curricular constraints contribute to this. Schools who are committed to their children's creative endeavours prioritize opportunities for extended and in-depth work, and identify particular times when this will happen, but how exactly this is done will depend on individual circumstances.

The Place of Talk

Collaborative tasks and other opportunities for talk provide excellent opportunities for creativity. In collaborative tasks, each individual offers a slightly different perspective on the task and such ideas can promote further ideas from within the group. By having so many ideas around and differing perspectives on these ideas, the group can readily develop new ideas and perspectives. Further, the opportunities provided for group members to misinterpret each others' contributions allows for even greater creativity. This is also the case for discursive enquiries. By internalizing these creative dialogues, children leave such discussions with an improved capacity to engage in similar creative inner dialogues by themselves.

Such activities, together with their engagement in decision-making in class and through bodies such the school council, allow children to make real choices and be consulted on changes. As such they promote autonomous, self-directed and independent learners. Teachers who are sensitive to their role in the classroom can support such learners without over-controlling and therefore stifling this autonomy. As has been said already, in these classes teachers need to:

- emphasize discussion and the sharing and exploration of ideas;
- seek and explore alternative ways of looking at things;
- create an atmosphere where risk-taking is acceptable and mistakes are considered to be opportunities for learning;
- value freedom of expression provided it does not set out to deliberately upset or offend.

Assessment and Creativity

Assessment has a key role in promoting thoughtful approaches by children. If we adopt approaches to assessment which value children's contributions when they attempt to be original and adopt fresh perspectives, then in so doing we will encourage these. Of course, to allow children to do this we must encourage autonomy by:

- allowing them to make choices about the theme, focus and goals of their work;

- encouraging them to plan their own work and evaluate their own success;

- encouraging them to use a variety of genres, styles and forms of representation in their work (for example, drawing, painting, writing, drama);

- providing them with a variety of quality resources from which they can choose, and teach them about the various resources provided so that they care for them, use them appropriately and select the right tool for the job;

- publicly celebrating the range of approaches adopted in assemblies, displays and the like.

Creativity and Disciplined Thinking

Providing children with meaningful and purposeful activities and allowing them to work with experts encourages them to see the world in particular ways. Thus working together on water-colour landscape paintings with a local artist helps children not only to learn the skills of using watercolours and painting landscapes, but also to begin to see the world as a painter. The exhibition of resulting paintings provides an authentic purpose for this activity.

Such activities teach children to see the world in different ways. Having done this they can look at the same area of learning from various perspectives, for example, looking at their local environment through a consideration of its geographical features, from an environmental perspective, and from a historical perspective using watercolour paintings, drama, music and so on to represent their ideas. Such an approach allows for the creative combination of ideas and forms of representation.

Developing this further, the connectedness of ideas can also be considered: how is the historical perspective linked to the geographical or environmental one, and how does it differ? Indeed, how do conceptual ideas such as those in science link to the emotions of, say, environmental activists? Cross-curricular thematic studies provide opportunities for this work. Popular and established approaches such as planning using topic webs, and arranging themed days and even weeks of activities are entirely appropriate here, despite the complaint from some that they lack rigour.

Through this work we are aiming to develop in children the ability to adopt particular perspectives on issues, but to be able to change to other perspectives as well, and by dancing between perspectives be able to develop creative solutions to problems. In encouraging this, teachers need to:

- go beyond the formal curriculum;

- focus on first-hand experience and active learning;

- present ideas in alternative ways, for example, using drama in science or the humanities;

- integrate learning across the curriculum in thematic studies;

- make learning tasks meaningful and purposeful;

- explore learning in real-life contexts and take learning out of the classroom, making use of out of school links and community expertise.

The Issue of Relevance

The foregoing sections focus, to a great extent, on the need for children to engage in meaningful and relevant work. To be such, it should make use of the local features and issues which form a part of the children's worlds of experience. It should also respond to their current interests, experiences and to current events, acknowledging previous experiences and events, and in so doing help children to make sense of their world. By making the curriculum in which children engage directly relevant to their lives beyond school we are more likely to engage their thinking purposefully.

CASE STUDY

Invaders and Settlers

In Chapter 1 I mentioned a research study that I carried out concerning children's learning in different activities. In this work year 6 children looked at the Saxons as an example of invaders and settlers. A similar programme of study was developed with a group of year 3 and 4 children, and some of this is described in the Case Study of archaeology in the classroom in Chapter 4. As well as their archaeological experience of historical enquiry the children also engaged in:

- literacy lessons based on texts on social and domestic arrangements in Saxon settlements, which also described the use of archaeological evidence;

- history lessons in which the children used a selection of texts and websites, provided by their teacher, to gather information about particular aspects of social life in Saxon times and the evidence for this, and used this information to create their own accounts;

- drama lessons in which children developed ideas with their teacher whilst enacting roles set in a Saxon village;

- other historical enquiries following on from their work with the archaeologist.

The children were allowed to work for extended periods in each of these areas, and a considerable proportion of their work involved hands-on investigation, exploration and research, followed by discussions of findings. The experiences of people in Saxon times were represented in various ways: the children worked on writing narratives and poems, on drawing and painting, and refined their work in drama into a performance. The resulting work showed considerable imagination and sensitivity in relating the lives of Saxons long ago to the children's lives now.

CASE STUDY

National Parks

National parks provide a rich source of first-hand work in many areas: this Case Study could have considered history, looking again at archaeology, considering religious and spiritual themes such as myths and legends, the impact of early Christianity on the region, and so on.

However such a study also provides an excellent context for environmental work. A year 5 class spent half a term working on such a theme, incorporating a residential visit into their study. During the visit children explored the local environment in many ways using all their senses – and recorded their explorations in many ways as well, using writing, art, music, dance and so on.

One aspect of the children's work involved exploring what a national park is. They interviewed local people, visitors and national park wardens to find out what the positive and negative effects of being a national park were for the environment. Together they discussed their findings and came to conclusions about what they had found out. Finally, they used all their explorations and work to produce a display in a local visitor centre entitled 'National Parks: Past, Present and Future'.

The range of approaches described above is listed and illustrated in Task 5.3 as an audit which you can use in your class or school. The suggestion is that environments which support the development of creative dispositions and which provide creative opportunities for children contain many of the features listed. In this chapter I am not suggesting that we can teach children to be creative: rather that schools can allow them to be so by the way they are organized.

Connections Everywhere

In this chapter I have argued that a key outcome of developing approaches which encourage children to use their thinking skills in the primary school is that children have more opportunities to be creative. Indeed, most of the approaches suggested in this book – collaborative group

Lesson Ideas (with a suggested Thinking Skills Emphasis): Exploring Themes Through Different Media

Using a fable, traditional folk tale, or even a poem, work of art or piece of music as a starting point, the story and events are interpreted and reinterpreted through drama, dance and music. This culminates in the children performing their different representations, perhaps one after the other or perhaps integrating all into one performance, for a local audience. (*Possible Thinking Skills Emphasis: being creative*)

Following a dramatic exploration of life cycles and food webs, based on North European deciduous woodland and following a field trip to such woodland, the children write poems based on the experiences of particular animals, imagining themselves to be those animals. Other media are also used to create representations, including collage, and finally the children write stories based on their understandings and experiences. (*Possible Thinking Skills Emphasis: being creative*)

Task 5.3(a) Auditing and planning for a creative curriculum (prompt questions)

Use the prompts to complete the blank creativity audit for your class (Task 5.3 (b)).

Focus on first-hand experience and active learning ■ How passive are the children in your classroom? ■ What is the place of 'doing' and activity in learning? ■ Are children taught actively to listen and read?	**Allow children to make real choices and be consulted on changes** ■ Do you have a school council? ■ Do children have opportunities to decide: their approach to problems; what they will learn? ■ Are children consulted on changes? ■ What is the role of self-assessment and evaluation in your classroom?	**Emphasize discussion and the sharing and exploration of ideas** ■ Do you use circle times? ■ Do the children discuss complex (for example, moral) issues? ■ Are children allowed time to think before responding? ■ Are debates extended over several days? ■ Do teachers consider their use of questioning strategies?	**Create an atmosphere where risk-taking is OK and mistakes are considered to be opportunities for learning** ■ What is the balance between summative and formative assessment in your classroom? ■ To what extent are children aware of and involved in their own formative assessment? ■ Is there a policy on correcting mistakes? ■ How are children encouraged to learn from errors, mistakes or misconceptions? ■ Do teachers take risks?
Use tasks which involve collaboration and co-operation ■ To what extent is co-operative group work used in your classroom? ■ Are children assigned roles in groups depending on their strengths? ■ To what extent are individuals accountable in group tasks? ■ Do individuals have clear tasks in co-operating towards a group outcome?	**Explore learning in real-life contexts, look at subjects in action and make out-of-school links** ■ Is the metaphor for your classroom a production line, or is it an artist's studio, a scientist's lab, a writer's workshop, and so on?	**Integrate learning across the curriculum in thematic studies, making links clear** ■ Are links made using topic webs? ■ To what extent are full day activities and themed weeks used?	**Present ideas in alternative ways, for example, using drama, music, and so on in subjects such as science or humanities** ■ Are concepts and ideas presented in various different ways?
Seek and explore alternative ways of looking at things ■ Do children take a view on an issue as a scientist, as a historian, and so on? ■ Do they try to work as these people might? ■ Do children consider alternative viewpoints? ■ Do children write the same piece from different perspectives, create alternative explanations, and so on? ■ Do you use role-play for children to explore different roles?	**Go beyond the curriculum** ■ Is your work limited to the National Curriculum? ■ Do you use: drama; some 'child chosen' themes; local studies (for example, lace making), current issues, and so on?	**Take learning out of the classroom** ■ How do the school grounds contribute to learning? ■ How do trips and visits contribute to learning?	**Make use of community and other expertise** ■ Do you regularly have local or other experts in school, for example artists, authors, poets, local historians, and so on?
Make learning tasks meaningful and purposeful, and activities authentic; for example, make performance and exhibition central to the arts ■ What do children think their learning at school is for? ■ To what extent is the focus on working, and to what extent is it on learning? **Recognize the place of the performing and creative arts** ■ What part do the creative and expressive arts play in your timetable? ■ Are children involved in regular productions, and do they write, plan, stage manage and direct these? ■ Is creative work varied: ceramic, painting and drawing, textiles, and so on; and are the results exhibited? ■ Are poetry anthologies, and so on produced?	**Allow for flexibility in the curriculum** ■ Do timetable restraints affect your teaching? ■ What is the place of learning in clubs and 'out-of-hours' activities?		

Using Thinking Skills in the Primary Classroom © Kelly, 2005

Task 5.3(b) Auditing and planning for a creative curriculum (response sheet)

Focus on first-hand experience and active learning	Use tasks which involve collaboration and co-operation	Allow children to make real choices and be consulted on changes	Emphasize discussion and the sharing and exploration of ideas	Create an atmosphere where risk-taking is OK and mistakes are considered to be opportunities for learning
Make learning tasks meaningful and purposeful, and activities authentic; for example, make performance and exhibition central to the arts	Seek and explore alternative ways of looking at things	Explore learning in real-life contexts, look at subjects in action and make out-of-school links	Integrate learning across the curriculum in thematic studies, making links clear	Present ideas in alternative ways, for example, using drama, music, and so on in subjects such as science or humanities
Recognize the place of the performing and creative arts	Allow for flexibility in the curriculum	Go beyond the curriculum	Take learning out of the classroom	Make use of community and other expertise

Using Thinking Skills in the Primary Classroom © Kelly, 2005

work, discursive enquiry, critically reflective self-assessment, disciplined thinking and authentic activity – to some extent depend on that creativity. The case studies provided in the previous chapter could apply equally to this chapter in relation to developing children's creative dispositions. Thus, as with other considerations in this book, the approach is holistic. Unlike many educational initiatives which see the whole as merely the sum of a series of teachable parts, here is a whole which is considerably more than the bringing together of separate skills or approaches. In this connected approach to learning, the learning of teachers is inseparable from the learning of students, and it is to this that I turn in the final chapter.

Key Points

1. In this book I adopt the National Advisory Committee on Creative and Cultural Education's view of creativity as 'imaginative activity fashioned so as to produce outcomes that are both original and of value'.

2. To develop children who approach solving problems as original thinkers we should encourage them to be enquiring, active and autonomous learners.

3. Learners who have intellectual autonomy think for themselves, link their thinking to their experiences and open their minds to new ideas.

4. Schools committed to their children's creative endeavours prioritize opportunities for extended and in-depth work, and identify particular times when this will happen.

5. In emphasizing discussion and the sharing and exploration of ideas, teachers should seek and explore alternative ways of looking at things, create an atmosphere where risk-taking is acceptable and mistakes are considered to be opportunities for learning, and value freedom of expression provided it does not set out to deliberately upset or offend.

6. To allow children to be original and adopt fresh perspectives in their work we must encourage autonomy.

7. The activities teachers plan for their children should:
   (a) go beyond the formal curriculum;
   (b) focus on first-hand experience and active learning;
   (c) present ideas in alternative ways, for example, using drama in science or the humanities;
   (d) integrate learning across the curriculum in thematic studies;
   (e) make learning tasks meaningful and purposeful;
   (f) explore learning in real-life contexts and take learning out of the classroom, making use of out of school links and community expertise.

8. For the curriculum to be meaningful and relevant to children it must:
   (a) make use of those local features and issues which form a part of children's worlds of experience;
   (b) respond to their current interests, experiences and to current events, whilst acknowledging previous experiences and events;
   (c) in so doing, help children to make sense of their world.

CHAPTER 6

The Thinking School

From Classroom to School to Community

In this book I have provided a framework of related approaches which encourage children's deep engagement in their learning in the primary school. Throughout, the focus has been on using children's thinking skills in the primary classroom. But classes do not work in isolation – they are each part of a learning community, and learning is more powerful if it is reinforced through approaches across the whole of that community. In this chapter I discuss the need, once we have introduced thoughtful approaches in our classes, for us to move beyond the thinking classroom towards a thinking school and, ultimately, into a thinking community.

Reflection Point

One Conversation, One Perspective

Not long ago I was sitting in the office of a headteacher, Lesley, at the end of the school day. I had gone to run an after-school staff training session, but it had been cancelled due to staff illness.

Lesley: This is a school which enjoys tremendous support from parents and members of our local community and the children who come here are advantaged in many ways: by anyone's measure they are children who should be doing well. And yet I am not convinced that they work as hard as they might and that they all have that real spark of excitement with their learning. More often they seem to do just enough to get by – and it feels as though that's as much as they want.

Peter: And yet I bet there are areas out of school which really do interest and involve them.

Lesley: Yes. Do you know we have a girl in year 4 who is the regional chess champion for her age group, and yet it was only when she brought the trophy into school a few weeks ago that we found out she could even play chess!

Peter: But the parents are full of praise for what you all do here – even this evening, as I arrived I overheard some talking at the gate saying how well their children were doing here.

Lesley: Oh, the parents are happy, and on the face of it the school is doing well – each year our published test results are good, and we had an excellent Ofsted inspection last year.

Peter: Do staff share your unease?

Lesley: Some do. Joanna who's in year 1 is looking at how she can encourage children to keep their sense of purpose, curiosity and creativity as they move from the Foundation Stage through Key Stage 1, but she's finding it hard. And I've got a teacher in year 3 who wants to look at how she can make better use of drama in literacy. But many of the other teachers say there's no issue: if our results are good and Ofsted's happy, then what's the worry! I think they've got a point, and I can't ask them to do any more ... with staff meetings on Mondays, team planning on Tuesdays and for some senior management team meetings on Wednesdays ... they all work incredibly hard.

Peter: What about the thinking skills initiative that you've been involved in. You said everyone was keen on that. And the parent's workshop with the Local Education Authority adviser went really well, didn't it?

Lesley: Yes, that started well, but it's so hard to sustain these things with so many other pressures on people as well. We were finding that the thinking skills approaches which we tried were alright in the short term, but after their novelty value had worn off it was so hard to sustain them. Of course, some of the approaches are quite shallow, but the really worthwhile ones require such a commitment. Anyway, it's going to be number one priority in our development plan next year.

The Strategic Profession

The extract from a conversation in the Reflection Point above illustrates some of the key themes which have been raised and considered in this book: many of the children in our schools are predominantly strategic learners, doing just enough to meet the requirements of their parents and teachers and thus keeping everyone happy. That children are doing this is obscured because parents, and to some extent teachers, rely on externally imposed (in that they are done to rather than done with or by the school or children) and objective indicators (in the form of test results and inspection reports) to judge the success of the school – indicators which reflect the extent to which children are meeting the requirements of their parents and teachers! This is a state of affairs which conspires to marginalize deep learning.

But what is also interesting here is that many teachers at such schools also appear to have adopted a strategic attitude to their own professional practice which I will call a strategic professionalism: the pressure of work means that they direct their efforts almost entirely into meeting the externally imposed requirements. This also means that they are somewhat reliant on external solutions to problems – be they government strategies or, in this case, particular programmes. However, such programmes require commitment if they are to succeed, and commitment stems from ownership. Without commitment and ownership, the implementation of such programmes is likely to be somewhat 'hit and miss', and extremely frustrating for all involved.

Within this book I have provided guidance on the areas which teachers might address in their own contexts and some of the approaches that they might use if they are to encourage children to use their thinking skills and engage more deeply in their learning. These suggestions have included:

- increasing the role of classroom discussion and collaborative group work across the school;

- using a broad and participative approach to assessment;

- tackling the pressures of content overload and time by focusing on certain 'big ideas' and going for quality rather than quantity;

- adopting thematic, linked and contextual approaches to curriculum design;

- encouraging pupil autonomy.

I suggest that these approaches are as salient for teacher development as they are for pupil development.

The Thinking Teacher

As teachers we are subject to many of the same pressures as our students. Thus, when the pressure of workload is high and the degree of accountability great, we adopt strategic approaches in our own thinking and work with the sole intention of meeting externally imposed requirements. But thinking schools need thinking teachers, and children need models of deep thinking if they too are to engage in deep thinking. Such teachers, who adopt what I will call a deep professionalism, focus on understanding and improving student learning.

We might ask how we encourage teachers to adopt a deep rather than a strategic professionalism. The preceding chapters suggest that the solution lies in the following areas:

- increasing opportunities for staff discussion and collaborative school development initiatives across the school;

- using broad and complex success indicators in the process of teacher performance management rather than simple and measurable ones, whilst maintaining a strong emphasis on teachers' reflections and professional self-appraisal;

- tackling workload pressures by identifying and focusing on only a few key developments across the school each year, and going for quality rather than quantity;

- as a school tackling the pressures of curriculum content overload and time by identifying and focusing on key areas of learning for each year group and each subject, again going for quality rather than quantity;

- making links with outside agencies and maintaining an open and supportive dialogue with parents and members of the community;

- encouraging teacher innovation and enquiry.

I briefly consider these under three headings: teacher discourse and collaborative school cultures; professional reflection; and teacher enquiry.

Teacher Discourse and Collaborative School Cultures

It is worth returning to Task I.1 in the introductory chapter of this book. Considered in the terms of that task, strategic professional approaches have more in common with the industrial production line than with self-directed teams. Yet the deeper professionalism engaged in by those teams is more likely to meet strategic goals and provide a sounder basis for long-term development, whilst also satisfying the deeper needs of teachers.

To promote a deeper professionalism it is vital, therefore, that we increase opportunities for teachers to engage in reflection, collaborative work and critical discussions. Such work needs to occur both within and beyond the school community, and might include collaborations with other schools, local industries, universities and colleges, but also needs to embrace a dialogue with parents and members of the local community about local educational issues. It is through the latter that innovative and locally appropriate solutions to particular educational problems might be found.

However, those involved in working with children – teachers, teaching assistants, other school staff, parents and helpers – also need to embrace an educational dialogue with children which will serve to improve their own understanding alongside children's learning. That dialogue builds on approaches suggested in this book, and views adults and children as being learners alongside each other. It involves the kind of learning partnerships exemplified in the notion of a learning community.

Professional Reflection

A central feature of deep professionalism is a desire to engage in a critically reflective appraisal of one's own practice, focusing on understanding and improving student learning. Here the drive to improve comes from within. School structures need to support and even promote this drive – by encouraging teacher self-appraisal and peer appraisal, and by acknowledging the place of self-evaluation and reflection within the school's process of performance management. Many of the approaches to assessment suggested for children in Chapter 3 are relevant here, including the usefulness of professional journals or diaries and the importance of using teacher portfolios as a basis for engaging in critical reflection.

Similarly, there is a need for schools to develop and use complex ways of evaluating teacher performance, which examine those aspects of success which we really value as teachers. This might include an emphasis on changes in student attitude in a cohort over a period of time rather than simply looking for an improvement in the children's test results, which is, of course, much easier to access.

Teacher Enquiry

Coupled with the professional need for critical reflection is the desire to make changes and evaluate their impact. This is where the process of teacher enquiry supports reflective practice, but by adopting it within a collaborative school culture it can also be an effective approach to whole-school improvement.

However, teacher enquiry should not only focus on practice within the teacher's particular classroom in their particular school and community. Teachers involved in enquiry should reach out to use and evaluate ideas and approaches suggested by other teachers and researchers: in turn, they should have opportunities to share their findings with a wider audience and, in so doing, they can contribute towards the enquiry dialogues of local and wider research communities.

The Thinking School

But promoting thinking amongst both children and adults in a school community is not enough. To be a thinking community all must have opportunities to think together, and to reach out and think with members of the wider community. Here are a few ideas:

■ Promote democratic decision-making within the school through class councils and/or a whole-school council, which includes both pupils and adult representation. Members would have to be elected and represent their electorate. Councils could consider issues of policy (such as playtime organization) and should have a clear remit. They might call expert witnesses (such as pupils who had been to other schools and seen how their playtimes had been organized, meal-time assistants, teachers or parents), and would ultimately vote on decisions, decide how these should be carried out, evaluate their success and review progress.

■ Extend this democratic decision-making involvement to setting up class/school courts – based on a reconciliatory notion rather than an adversarial one. Perhaps every child could, at some time, have a turn at being a juror. Such courts would be forums seeking the truth about allegations of misbehaviour and reconciliation for those involved.

■ Involve class/school councils in staff appointments – perhaps even have a pupil interview panel.

■ Engage in whole-school collaborative ventures across year groups with school staff and members of the community working alongside children – for example a poetry week resulting in the production of an anthology of poetry from across the whole school and a poetry reading event for children and members of the local community to take part in. Here it is important that class and school boundaries are opened – children working with others of different ages and with adults. Other ventures might include a community orchestra involving both children and adults and jointly planned community performances and events.

■ Thoroughly exploit the many opportunities for celebrating the widest achievements of all within the school and community in an open and inclusive forum – so that the success of each individual is shared and enjoyed by all, and any success which the school enjoys is also seen as a success for the local community.

Schools as Learning Communities for All

The approaches to promoting student thinking and learning which form the basis of this book are greatly connected to ways of improving teachers' reflective thinking and professional learning. Some suggest that the achievement of these goals lies in skills training for all: whether thinking skills training for students or competency training for teachers. However, as I hope I have shown in this book, the teaching of isolated skills or competencies, taken out of context, is unlikely to promote deep-seated and lasting changes. Rather, the solution lies in all members of the school community and surrounding locality being lifelong learners collectively engaging in solving shared problems and enjoying shared successes, and thereby promoting schools as learning communities for all.

Key Points

1. Teachers are subject to many of the same pressures as their students. Thus the pressures of workload and accountability encourage a 'strategic professionalism' which focuses on meeting externally imposed requirements.

2. Teachers with a 'deep professionalism' focus on understanding and improving student learning. To encourage this schools must:

   (a) value and promote opportunities for staff discourse and collaborative school development, and extend this to productive discourses and collaborations beyond the school community;

   (b) use broad indicators in teacher performance management, and maintain a strong emphasis on teachers' professional appraisal;

   (c) develop a clarity of focus and emphasis on quality rather than quantity to tackle workload pressures and the curricular pressures of content overload;

   (d) encourage teacher innovation and enquiry.

3. Schools where students intend to understand and where teachers focus on understanding and improving student learning are learning communities for all.

4. To be a thinking community all members of that community — children, teachers, teaching assistants and parents — must have opportunities to think together, and to reach out and think with members of the wider community.

Notes

Chapter 1

1. This reasearch is described in Noel Entwistle's chapter 'Contrasting perspectives on learning', in Marton, F., Hounsell, D. and Entwistle, N. (eds) (1997) *The Experience of Learning*. Edinburgh: Scottish Academic Press.
2. Carl Bereiter's work in Canada is described in Bereiter, C. (1990) 'Aspects of an educational learning theory', *Review of Educational Research*, vol. 60, pp. 603–24, and in the UK context a study by Charles Desforges and Anne Cockburn is described in Desforges, C. and Cockburn, A. (1987) *Understanding the Mathematics Teacher*. London: Falmer.
3. Taken from Department for Education and Employment (1999) *The National Curriculum: Handbook for Primary Teachers in England*. London: DFEE/QCA, p. 60.
4. These are reviewed in Prosser, M. and Trigwell, K. (1997) 'Relations between perceptions of the teaching environment and approaches to teaching', *British Journal of Educational Psychology*, vol. 4, pp. 513–28.
5. These are reported in Marton, F., Dall' Alba, G and Beaty, E. (1993) 'Conceptions of learning', *International Journal of Educational Research*, vol. 19, pp. 277–300.
6. Goldhagen, Daniel (1997) *Hitler's Willing Executioners: Ordinary Germans and the Holocaust*. London: Abacus.

Chapter 2

1. Taken from the National Primary Strategy document, QCA (2003) *Speaking and Listening Handbook*. London: QCA, p. 3.

Chapter 3

1. Adapted from Biggs, John and Collis, Kevin (1982) *Evaluating the Quality of Learning: The SOLO Taxonomy*. London: Academic Press.
2. Doyle, W (1983) Academic Work, Review of Educational Research 53(2) p. 181.

Chapter 5

1. National Advisory Committee on Creative and Cultural Education (2000) *All Our Futures: Creativity and Culture in Education*. London: DfES, p. 29.
2. See Bobbit-Nolan, Susan (1995) 'Teaching for autonomous learning', in C. Desforges (ed.), *An Introduction to Teaching: Psychological Perspectives*. Oxford: Blackwell.

INDEX

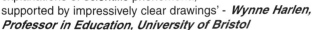